NORTHERN SPAIN

Cedric Salter

NORTHERN SPAIN

B. T. Batsford Ltd
London & Sydney

First published 1975
Copyright © Cedric Salter, 1975

ISBN: 0 7134 2896 1

Printed in Great Britain by
Richard Clay (The Chaucer Press) Limited, Bungay, Suffolk
for the publishers
B. T. Batsford Ltd, 4 Fitzhardinge Street, London W1
and 23 Cross Street, Brookvale, NSW 2100, Australia

Contents

Acknowledgements

The publishers gratefully acknowledge the kind permission of the Spanish National Tourist Office to reproduce photographs 2, 4–9, 13, 15–18, 20, 22, 25, 27. Nos 1 and 12 are reproduced by arrangement with Anne Bolt, nos 11 and 26 by arrangement with Allan Watson, nos 19, 21 and 24 by arrangement with A. F. Kersting and nos 3, 10, 14, 23 by arrangement with J. Allan Cash.

List of Illustrations

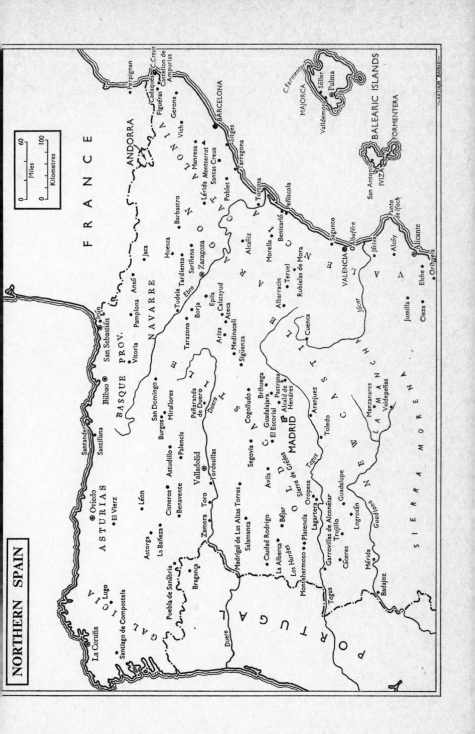

NORTHERN SPAIN

This book is for

The Right Honourable Selwyn Lloyd, C.H., M.P.

A MAN FOR ALL SEASONS

in gratitude for his great patience
and many kindnesses

Introduction

I had the good fortune to know Spain before the world tourist invasion began – in fact I must confess that I bear some slight guilt for having started it by books and articles published as long ago as the very early 1950s. The result has been to bring a wave of prosperity to the country but – like most good deeds – to destroy some, though by no means all, of the things that first attracted me.

Understandably, the great developers exploited northern Europe's almost desperate need for sun, sandy beaches and a reasonably warm sea for bathing which, until the pound went a-floating, they could provide inexpensively. Today they have more or less taken over the entire Mediterranean coast and Balearic Islands, and reinforced the hold they always possessed over Seville and most of Andalucia. More recently they have turned their attention to Madrid, with the ring of fascinating and ancient cities which surround it, for those with a more urban taste in holidays.

This is much – but Spain is a far bigger country than most people seem to realise. Nor am I suggesting that all the changes have been for the worse. Many people are delighted to run into their London, Manchester or Glasgow next-door neighbours on the Costa de Fish y Chips – and why not? My point is that, in addition to the born package tourist, there are still a surprisingly large number of people who might like to visit Spanish Spain, and it still exists behind the brassy façade of the Costas.

As I, and many others, have often remarked, there are several Spains which, by some potent trick of Ibero–Celtic magic, exist simultaneously, as if on different levels of consciousness, which somehow never seriously overlap one another. I cannot explain it but, as I have said, I am by no means the only person who has become aware of it.

There is still a large, unchanged, fifteenth- to eighteenth-century

Spain, and considerable pockets of a mediaeval one, into which you can effortlessly drift if you care to do so. This emphatically does not mean a world of 'roughing it' amid the dubious delights of faulty plumbing, wandering hippies and decaying monasteries – I am always firmly in favour of a reasonable degree of physical comfort – and the purpose of this book is only to lead you into this more tranquil and more ancient Spain which still remains, and will always remain, secure in its secret strongholds.

So I write here of the foothills of the Pyrenees, with their upland meadows thickly sprinkled with autumn crocuses and mushrooms, and of the lower passes through which, in October, the migratory pigeons come flooding south from their Baltic breeding grounds on their way to northern Africa. It is a place of countless bright streams singing over their incredibly clear, pebbled beds, where speckled trout are still plentiful, and of rickety storks' nests perched askew on crumbling terracotta tiled roofs, and of warm, sturdily built stone houses for comfort and rest at the end of the day.

But that is not all, for soon we come through mountain ways to a green, northern sea which has cut fjord-like inlets into the defiant coast, and join the greatest of all the mediaeval pilgrim ways, to Santiago de Compostela. This winds through Burgos, where lies the body of El Cid Campeador, passes the prehistoric cave paintings of Altamira, and brings us to that vast glowing lamp of the Faith which is the matchless stained-glass Cathedral of Leon. We slip south for a while to visit the mighty University of Salamanca before ending our quest at the Tomb of St James the Apostle, cousin of Christ, son of Zeberde and Salome and elder brother of St John the Evangelist, which lies in the land of the Golden Legend.

This carries you through a part of the ancient Spain of history and ancient memories, passing the Caves of Covadonga from which Pelayo led his small, dedicated band of Christian knights, and launched the 700-year-long Crusade that finally expelled the once all-conquering hordes of Islam from Spanish soil in the very same year in which Columbus sailed from a Spanish port to discover America.

We shall meet tourists in passing, and if we reach our destination in Santiago de Compostela – the *campus stellae*, or starry field – around July 24th, we shall find thousands of fellow-pilgrims but for the most part we shall be moving through a countryside and among a people which have changed only superficially with the centuries. Here, still, is the real Spain.

2   *Our Lady of Solitude, carried by penitents on a Holy Day*

3   *Fingers of rock above the Monastery of Montserrat. Here, once, the Holy Grail was hidden in a cave*

1. Barcelona and the Catalan Pyrenees

To me Barcelona happens to be a city of many memories. When I was there on holiday in July of 1936, still very young, I became involved in my first assignment as a foreign correspondent – the Spanish Civil War. What I then thought would be just an exciting, and much-needed, job for a month or two developed into nine grim years as a war correspondent, for there was only a brief pause between Franco's final victory and my arrival in Warsaw to observe the outbreak of World War Two, and it changed the entire course of my life more completely than any other single event.

It was odd today to sit in front of the same little pavement café at which I sat on that fateful morning long ago, and on many subsequent mornings, and to watch the prosperous holiday crowds go by; and then to remember this same street, then shell and bomb-scarred, and the grey-faced few who straggled by, some fearful, others fanatic, but all hungry.

But this is not an autobiography, and my excuse for recalling such things is that everywhere in Spain the barrier between the years, even between the centuries has, for me, always been uncannily transparent, for here all time is eternal so that the past can become more real than the present, and only the future is hidden in the womb.

So it was to this well-remembered yet strange city that my jet plane today delivered me in no time at all, where first I had arrived sitting on a very hard, wooden third-class railway carriage seat, with less than a pound in the world, eating the last of my three-days-old sandwiches and drinking the last of my buvette-bought, old two pence worth bottle of heartening red Catalan wine, an age ago. It was pleasant to see it again, now as then, for it will always be, for me, 'the place where it all began'.

Although I may sound so, I am not particularly sentimental about places just because they are familiar, and sentimental pilgrimages have always turned out to be disastrous. There are, in fact, a large number of familiar towns that I never wish to see again, such as Basra, Baghdad, Sofia, Warsaw, Rangoon and Luanda to mention only a few, but Barcelona, though it teems a bit these days, is for me a good place from which to begin another journey.

It was so long ago since I lived, first here, and then at what was the still unspoiled little fishing village of Sitges, that it seemed as though it belonged to an earlier life, and still longer since I last made my way to the top of Tibidabo – the great hill that dominates this magnificent Mediterranean port of two and a half million people and (may I add) a very 'trippery' kind of thing to do anyway!

You must never think of these two and a half million, or their less urban compatriots, as Spaniards. They are Catalans, with their own language, literature, poetry, music, history and folk dances, and their stately *sardana* is, in my opinion, the loveliest of all Iberian folk-dances, with its sharp, reedy music to pace the concentric circles of the performers.

The spreading city is a fascinating sight seen from the summit of Tibidabo, and from it, once in a long while, you can glimpse a shadow on the farthest sea-horizon which is Majorca or Menorca. South, too, one looks towards Roman Tarragona only 40-odd miles, but shut away by the sea-cliffs known as the Costas de Garraf. To the north, at any time of the year except early autumn, there is a staggering view of the snow-capped Pyrenees, piling up to formidable 10,000 and 11,000 feet high peaks. Seen from this distance they look an even more imposing barrier than when you are, as we shall later be, close to them, and can perceive the fertile valleys and fir-clad slopes and passes with which they are threaded.

On this particular journey the less dramatic view inland is

also worth crossing Tibidabo's summit to see, for there lies the mountain monastery of Montserrat, with its petrified fingers pointing accusingly to heaven, clearly visible only 30 miles away, and rising almost sheer from the plain of the River Llobregat.

Of course, Montserrat's closeness to Barcelona has made it a major tourist attraction, with the consequent threat to its seclusion, but the aura of what to me has always seemed a faintly malevolent power emanating from the small Black Virgin in the dark church, is potent enough to subdue even the most exuberantly packaged tourist. If you are male, and have sought a permit in advance, you can pass the small door into the monastery itself, where the monks seem still to have preserved a certain degree of Shangri-La timelessness and mystery.

For mystery is still there – not in the monastery buildings but in the countless hidden caves of this fantastic out-thrust of rock.

In one of them – the mile-long tunnel which ends in the Santa Cueva ('Holy Cave') – the Black Virgin was safely hidden during the centuries of Moslem occupation. It was then that the smoke from the votive candles gradually darkened the once pale wood carved, tradition holds, by St Luke, but revealing Byzantine influences of the fifth or sixth centuries, and in another the Holy Grail was at long last found by Parsifal.

In the small quiet garden of the monastery voices float up to you from 3,700 feet below – human voices, crying and singing, raised in laughter or in tears – but whether they are the voices of those who lived yesterday or of those who live today it is sometimes difficult to be sure.

Since everything about this strange place is linked, directly or indirectly, with the story of the Black Virgin I should perhaps finish what I have begun. After her long period in the Santa Cueva she was enthroned and much venerated by the Benedictine monks who established themselves on the Holy Mountain in A.D. 986 and, in due course, housed in the eleventh-century Chapel of St Michael. Pilgrims came from all over Europe, and the importance and wealth of the Abbey increased accordingly, providing at least one Pope to the Throne of St Peter in the person of Cardinal della Rovere, implacable enemy of the Spanish Borgia Pope Alexander VI. So great was its prestige that it was granted a kind of extraterritorial independence, with its own flag, rather like the present-day Vatican City State. The boys with the best singing voices in Spain are still sent to Montserrat to join the choir, in much the same way as the best from all Italy go to the Sistine Chapel, or, in England, to Magdalen College School in Oxford.

But, after nearly a thousand years, adversity overtook the devotees of the Black Virgin. First Napoleon's troops sacked and burned all the monastery buildings and then, during the Carlist Wars later in the century, the whole vast monastery treasure of gold and silver plate was taken to provide the contestants with the sinews of war. There were dark days, too, during the Civil War, and at the bottom of the monk's plateau garden, are the 14 graves of Montserrat's relatively modern martyrs, murdered by the Anarcho-Syndicalists from Barcelona in 1936.

If you have previously applied to the Padre Aposentador to stay a night or two, you will penetrate behind the scenes (but do not attempt it around April 27th or September 8th, when there is a series of festivals connected with the Black Virgin attended by many thousands of Catalan newly-weds); do not miss the matchless 100,000 volume library, containing the first books ever printed in Spain – the work of the Montserrat Press during the closing years of the fifteenth century.

The Holy Mountain of the 'Virgin Morena' is dotted with ruined hermitages dating from the thirteenth to sixteenth centuries, and honeycombed with caves used as places of worship not only during the Moslem occupation but, far earlier, after the collapse of Rome and before the Christianisation of Spain's Visigothic invaders. Others, without any religious associations, but filled with stalactites and stalagmites, can be reached by donkeys hired in the little village of Collbato, though I learned that this particular excursion has largely lost its former popularity. Probably the package tour agencies could not get a clear ruling of exactly how VAT should be applied to travel by donkey, or there were trade union problems about persuading the donkeys to accept the 'closed shop' principal relating to working unsocial hours.

By and large the buildings of Montserrat today are unremarkable, but the setting is one of the most awesome I have seen anywhere in the world.

There was a day in July 1936 when, from the roof of a friend's flat in Bonanova, we counted no less than 16 churches or religious buildings in Barcelona simultaneously on fire, and I myself witnessed some of the atrocities committed in the name of 'Freedom' upon monks, nuns and priests who, for the most part, were good and harmless people. Many superficial observers ascribe this Catalan church-burning complex to disillusionment with, and disbelief in, Catholicism.

Nothing could be farther from the truth, since it is obvious that no one bothers to destroy a thing of which he is not afraid, and no one is afraid of a thing in which he does not believe.

Perhaps a short incident from those far off days is not out of place in explaining this odd-seeming mixture of piety and church-burning. It occurred in August 1936, when a wild crowd, of which I was one, pressed into the Plaza de Cataluña to hear the great Anarchist leader Buenaventura Durruti make a speech. He concluded something like this – '... and I swear to you, I, Buenaventura Durruti, that I will not rest until every church in Spain has been burned to the ground, and the power of the Church lies finally and completely broken. And this' (crossing himself) 'I solemnly swear to you in the Name of the Father, Son and Holy Ghost.' No one present, except myself, thought that he had said anything in the least bit peculiar! In short, they do not destroy because they do not believe, but because they believe so completely, even, on occasions, against their own desires.

The jugular vein of Barcelona's day- and night-life is, and always has been the Ramblas – the wide shop- and tavern-lined avenue that leads down from the great central square of the Plaza de Cataluña to the port. A section of it is devoted to the flower sellers where the daily displays of the national flower, the carnation, pass description. Then there is a section for the sale of caged birds and other pets and, lower down, a quarter of a mile or so from the Plaza, is the chair-lined walk where, formerly, the unbelievably lovely ladies of the town used to

promenade in the exercise of the oldest profession in the world
– alas, no longer permitted so openly to display their wares.

Going down the Ramblas – a phrase which in the old days
had a special connotation – there are two turnings to the left,
one into the heart of the narrow alleys of the Barrio Chino, to
the rabbit-warren heart of the early nineteenth-century restaurant of Caracoles; the other into the quiet serenity of the
eighteenth-century Plaza Real, with its immensely tall imperial
palm trees sailing up into the bright sky.

It was in this eighteenth-century square – still something of
a backwater despite the presence of a few discreet but excellent restaurants – that I once attended the only public poets'
competition I have ever encountered.

In the centre were three judges on a dais, upon which
Barcelona's budding Byrons had to climb and read their effu-
sions to a crowd of several hundreds. When the poems were
bad – and they were, frequently, very bad – the crowd would
moan very slightly, and the judges would take another squirt
out of the wine-skin they were sharing. When they were good
– and two or three were excellent – you could have heard the
proverbial pin drop. But, Catalan poetry aside, the thing that
charmed me most was the system of prize-giving. The third
best was given a rose made of silver; the second best, a rose
made of gold, and the winner a perfect natural bloom!

Being of a cynical turn of mind, I enquired whether this did
not occasionally lead to the winner stoutly insisting that the
poem of his runner-up was really even better than his own, but
I was assured that to the first prize of the natural bloom was
added the proceeds of a silver collection!

Barcelona today is so large and tourist-conscious that I hesitate to recommend restaurants or particular dishes. Here you
can find anything from birds-nest to sharks-fin soup, or even
knitted nylon spaghetti. For me the little fishing port restaurants are the most authentic – but then I am a man of garlic
and acquainted with squid!

You will wander in Barcelona as much or as little as you
please – and if it is July or August it will be the latter, as
Barcelona's humid upper eighties and occasional nineties in the
shade are not conducive to extensive pavement strolling.

Nevertheless, Barcelona is a proud and ancient city, usually at loggerheads with the dictates of Castile or, later, Spain. As the Iberian Barcino it witnessed Hannibal moving northeast to strike at Rome for the mastery of the known world, and Greek and Phoenician traders were calling at the superb natural harbour long before the time of Christ's crucifixion.

This early town was centred round the site of the present large, but rather ordinary-seeming cathedral – La Seu, as the Catalans call it. Here was built first a Roman temple, then a palaeochristian basilica, and then yet again, an exquisite Romanesque cathedral. Only last century did a misguided civic pride – and the influx of vast fortunes from textiles – produce most of the present building. In it, fortunately, are conserved many traces of the earlier buildings, above all the cloisters, which are comparable to the best to be seen anywhere in all Spain or, according to many experts, even in all France as well.

More modern, but equally pleasing is the custom whereby the great space before the cathedral is emptied at noon every Sunday, except during Lent, for the dancing of the 'sardana' – that restrained, yet lilting dance which is so very much more difficult to perform than it appears to the uninitiated spectator.

The sixteenth-century baroque Palacio de los Virreyes de Cataluña is today used to house the archives of the Kingdom of Aragon, and the Palacio de la Diputación, once the seat of Catalonia's independent parliament (and centre of local power as late as the early days of 1939) is impressive, being reached by a magnificent stairway leading through a patio of orange and lemon trees. But there are still glimpses of the far older city provided by a Roman forum; a third-century church and a sixth-century palace, entered from the Calle de los Condes de Barcelona.

The Counts of Barcelona – the title of the father of the present heir to the throne of Spain – established an independent principality in the ninth century, over 650 years before the liberation of Granada, and as early as the eleventh century Ramon Berenguer I granted Catalonia's 'Usatges', a remarkably early example of something like a democratic constitution. In this city, too, the first code of European maritime laws was laid down as early as 1259, so the Catalans are understandably proud of their place in history before they were absorbed into the Kingdom of Aragon which, with the marriage of Ferdinand to Isabella of Castile, brought about their never very enthusiastic incorporation into a united Spain.

At the very bottom of the Ramblas is an imposing statue of Cristobal Colon – better known, for some reason or other, as Christopher Columbus – pointing vaguely towards Palma de Mallorca but, no doubt, meant to be saying the equivalent of America's nineteenth-century 'Go West Young Man'. This is built on the exact spot where Ferdinand and Isabella received him in June 1493 on his return from the discovery of what he believed to his dying day was China, or Cathay.

Of a city of two and a half million very tourist-conscious Catalans there is little new to say except in rather tedious detail. You will not be there long before you discover the expensive but magnificent shopping street of the Paseo de Gracia – always, even in prewar days, 20 per cent more expensive than Madrid due, perhaps, to a certain French influence where women's clothes are concerned.

The Catalan is a worker, which the Spaniard may, or may not be (and the Andaluz never is, if he can possibly help it), and Barcelona has always possessed a sense of vigour and purpose lacking, except of late, everywhere west of the Pyrenees. They claim that they pay three quarters of the taxes garnered from all Spain, and I should be inclined to believe them, though I would hazard a guess that their canniness probably means that they manage to avoid paying quite a lot more! They have often been likened to the Scots for their shrewd, hard-headed business sense and, like the Scots, they are less obviously forthcoming than, for example, the *madrillenos* (the natives of Madrid), but if they really accept you as a friend, then you can count on them for life.

Oddly enough this Catalan canniness is coupled with artistic ability of an exceptional order in many fields, particularly music, and the Liceo Opera House – though a product of bourgeois wealth of only a century or less ago – is second only to the Scala of Milan for size and splendour, and the gallery is always filled with lower paid workers who have probably cut a meal or two to buy their ticket, who follow each note on the

distant stage from battered musical scores, and stir with aud-
ible disapproval if some diva funks a high C – though it goes
unnoticed among the bank-vault-dimmed, diamond-encrusted
inmates of the family boxes, who would probably associate the
phrase with a rough day on the yacht!

The names of Gaudi in architecture, or Salvador Dalí, Sert
and Rusiñol in painting and Casals in music are evidence of
this rather surprising, innate Catalan aptitude for the arts and,
although born a *malagueño* (an inhabitant of Malaga), Barcelona was one of the formative influences upon Picasso.

Picasso and Barcelona have for me a slightly maddening
mental association, reminding me of a missed opportunity for
an affluent old age.

Before May 1937, when Barcelona was the scene of a particularly bloody revolution within a Civil War, and the central
Government, under Negrin, took control from the Catalan
separatist Government of Companys, there was one of those
odd local lulls which, I have since discovered, often occur during wars, and it was still safe to enjoy quite a deal of my
favourite outdoor sport of pavement café sitting. During such
a session I was approached by one of the numerous itinerant
salesmen who always haunt confirmed pavement-sitters, trying
to sell anything from 'feelthy pictures' to not very solid gold
rings. With the pillaging of the houses of compulsorily absent
(or shot) landlords, their offerings were occasionally interesting
in those days.

I absent-mindedly leafed through the usual collection offered
in a large, shabby, hard-backed black folder containing prints,
sketches and so on. There were the familiar, shiny prints of
pussy-cats playing winsomely with balls of wool, babies sitting
angelically on their pots to the adoring admiration of their
mothers, and the Spanish equivalent to our Vicar's daughter's
watercolour impression of the local 'view'. I then stopped
abruptly at a ten inch by six inch blue pastel drawing on
brownish paper.

It depicted a delightfully pert little lady of the town, waiting
to be 'picked up'. She had a very tall blue feather in her hat,
and her dress was *fin-de-siècle*. She looked fragile, flower-like,
very young, but obviously happy in her work. I tried not to

look too eager, and turned on a few more pages of the collection before returning to it. After a little ritual haggling I bought it for the modern equivalent of 75 pence. It was quite a lot of money in those days – but Picasso had, obligingly, signed it!

Two days later I went on leave to the south of France, where I had rented a magnificent furnished villa, in Mougins, not a mile from where Picasso was to die many years later, for £20 a month. It had a large garden, and being high on the hill in the direction of Grasse, had a splendid view over the Isles de Lerin. I had no difficulty in establishing that the sketch I had brought with me was genuine and, as was obvious, of the favoured 'blue period', and I sold it for the huge sum of £250 to a refugee Catalan lawyer. I was so pleased with my acumen that I dined out on the story for the rest of my leave. The last time it changed hands the newspapers said that the price was £28,000.

Unfortunately, I am not built to kick myself convincingly, though I have kept on trying to do so for half a lifetime!

Later, I took the plunge on Persian miniatures on ivory, when we temporarily took over Persia in 1941, and again in Macão with a pair of jade lions. After preserving these treasures against a rainy day through fire, war, earthquake and bomb, I disposed of both the other day for about one-half of what I had paid for them 30 years ago. Clearly my talents, if any, do not lie in the direction of a successful dealer in art!

But it is time to begin. We will avoid the Costa Brava to the northeast as I no habla Inglez very well. Nothing can quite ruin its physical beauty, but I knew it before it became a Crown and Anchor Colony so, except occasionally out of season, it gives me little joy today. Instead I suggest that we should aim due north, through the green foothills towards Puigcerdá, capital of the Cerdaña.

There is an electric railway all the way from Barcelona through Puigcerdá to Toulouse (with the obligatory change from the Spanish wide gauge to the French narrow one), which I used to employ during the summer months of the Civil War in preference to the more familiar route through Gerona and Figueras to Port Bou or, if by road, le Perthus. For one reason, in the height of summer the heat by the second route could be terrific whereas, at 3,000 feet or so it was bearable. Additionally, the French towns that follow the Puigcerdá route, such as Aix-les-Thermes and Foix in the Ariège are infinitely more attractive than Perpignan, Narbonne and Béziers. Carcassonne is a long way from both routes, so hardly affects the point.

On one such trip in the early days of the Civil War – undertaken, by the way, under a rota system for the stocking-up of tinned food and drinks for the entire British journalistic colony in Barcelona – I arrived at Puigcerdá and, having cleared the slightly trigger-happy customs and military police controls, I was waiting for the connection across the valley into French territory, when I was struck by a worried-looking Catalan family seated outside the little waiting-room and, over a drink, asked the customs chief just what they were doing there.

He replied, 'We were tipped off from Barcelona that they are smuggling out a fortune in jewels, and, if they are, we have orders to shoot them.'

'Well, why don't you search them?' I asked.

'Ah! but we have,' replied the douanier, 'and to the skin, but found nothing.'

'So what do you do now?' I queried.

With a sly grin the official said, 'I see that you don't know all the tricks the bloody capitalists are up to. Now we wait for the result of the big dose of castor oil to show us what valuables they may have swallowed. If that reveals nothing, then we shall let them go – but I think that it will.'

I looked again, with considerable sympathy at the family – father, wife, son and daughter, and meditated upon their singularly unhappy situation. No wonder they all wore the same careful, inward look of heroic constipation on their faces. Could they hope to win, if they were guilty, with time and castor oil as their remorseless enemies? If they failed they would lose their entire fortune in exile, even if they could buy their lives and escape. But there was nothing that I could do to help them, and I never found out what happened, as the daily train had arrived and I was forced to leave.

It is no doubt a somewhat eyebrow-lifting confession to my superior friends who go each year to Switzerland for winter sports and social uplift, but I prefer my mountains in the summer or early autumn, and the steady climb from Barcelona's unlovely outskirts to the green hills of Rodos, rising to over 3,000 feet just southwest of Vich, is one of the most exhilarating I have found anywhere. Soon poplars line the busy little streams, all flowing in the opposite direction – and if it is autumn those same poplars seem to retain their sun-coloured leaves intact until they look like a pale line of lighted, unflickering candle-flames.

Vich itself, only 40 miles from the Big City, already stands 1,575 feet above the Mediterranean and, in the shade, or at sunset, there is a subtle trace of coolness in the air even when Barcelona is a humid 95° F. It is not much more than a large village of 18,000 or so people, but has played a small part in history. Sacked by the Anarcho-Syndicalists in 1936, and knocked about by Napoleon's troops in 1810, the cathedral crypt dates from as early as 1038, and the cloisters and tower, known as 'El Cloquer', from 1180.

However, the most striking thing about the interior is the extraordinary murals of José Maria Sert, whose nephew Paco was my first friend when I went to live in Spain at the end of the 1939–45 war. The great Catalan painter, who died in that same year, had not quite finished his gigantic 'Mystery of the Redemption', but his sketches enabled his pupil, Miguel Massot, to complete it worthily.

The effect is slightly overwhelming as, in his last years, Sert became somewhat obsessed by the machinery of the human body, so that the spirituality of the concept seems to me to suffer in favour of a turgid striving of mighty masculine muscles – but it is unquestionably yet another example of the astonishing artistic heritage of the normally hard-headed, businesslike Catalans.

In the town there is the rather untidy ruin of a third century Roman temple where, until recently, stood the Moncada Palace, but I prefer my ruins slightly less ruinous – by which I mean that, after a certain point, the architectural conception as a whole becomes unreal to me or, I suspect, to anyone except an archaeologist.

Near by, too, are the remains of a castle of the Knights Templar, built in 1050, and various Lombardic churches of the eleventh and twelfth centuries approached, be it noted, over 'roads' which are often little more than sheep tracks and, even when you arrive, they are truly empty, all memory of power having long since faded into earth, sky and the pagan winds from the mountains.

But Vich is a highly prosperous little town, as is emphasised by its enormous, arcaded plaza – but its fame is founded, as it were, upon its sausages and smoked hams. Some of them seem a trifle strange at first to the Anglo-Saxon eye and palate, but they are, in fact, quite excellent – particularly if you are not allergic to a little garlic – and they are sold throughout Spain.

Inevitably the locals claim an old 'chestnut' as their own, but in case you have led a sheltered life, it relates to two manu-facturers of Vich sausages, one prosperous, the other im-poverished. When the latter asks how the former can sell his chicken sausages so cheaply and still make a profit, the successful one winks, and says,

'Well! dead donkeys are pretty cheap, why not mix it 50–50 with your chicken?' The unsuccessful man tries this, but re-turns a week later and reports that, even mixing donkey meat half-and-half with the chicken, he is still losing money. His successful friend replies scornfully,

'I didn't say mix the meats half-and-half, I said 50–50 – one donkey to one chicken.'

Certainly Vich's smoked mountain hams, often kept for seven or more years hanging are, when sliced wafer thin, quite delicious. They say that their mountain pigs grow a thick, nerveless pad on their snouts, so that when they are bitten by an adder during their non-stop rootling around for food, the snake's bite does not penetrate to the animal's blood-stream, and the pigs then proceed to gobble up the snake, thus acquir-ing a particularly delicious flavour – but this may, like the donkey mixture, be just another local myth!

Our road – and railway – now follow the brisk little River Ter, passing the ruined castles of Gurb and, later, Besora, which frowns down upon this frivolous age from a 3,000-foot peak which might have been designed as the lair of the evil sorcerer by Walt Disney, but, like most mediaeval castles, it looks far more romantic from below – except, of course, for the view from its walls.

Ripoll snuggles in the arm made by the junction of the River Fressner with the Ter, and the little town is chiefly known for its Benedictine Monastery founded by Count Wilfred in the year 888. It was consecrated in 935 and again, after a brief Moslem occupation, in 977. It was ravaged by fire in 1835, but restored with great fidelity and taste.

If you have a liking – as I must admit I have – for grotesque, Romanesque monsters, then you should take a look at the eleventh-century church housing the tombs of Count Borrell II, who died in 992, and King Ramon Berenguer III, who have rested there since 1113. You will find the monsters around the western door. In fact this is an area rich in Romanesque chapels, monasteries and abbeys, and I once deviated from Ripoll for the seven miles necessary to see a strange wooden twelfth-century calvary in San Juan de la Abadesas, locally known as *las Brujas* – 'the witches' – because of the terrifying figures it portrays.

From Ripoll the climb becomes a serious affair until we reach a 4,620 feet pass as a preliminary to dropping some 700 feet into the Cerdaña, or Cerdogne – which, for me, was once something of a private Shangri-La. It is difficult to realise it, but this enchanted valley is still less than 100 miles from Barcelona.

The little town stands high on a bluff (or, in Catalan, a *puig*) beside a lake which is loud with the love songs of a million or so oversexed bull-frogs! For the winter-sportsmen there are Masella, La Molina and Nuria near at hand, complete with chair-lifts, ski-lifts and cable cars to the 8,000-feet high slopes of Mount La Tossa or 10,000-feet Puigmal.

A pleasant oddity of Puigcerdá is that from it there is a 'neutral road' across a couple of miles of French territory to the Spanish enclave village of Lliria, where most of the 800 or so population have, since time immemorial, devoted themselves to the ancient and once romantic profession of smuggling. Until 1177 Lliria was the 'capital' of the Cerdogne but, through some quibble in the Treaty of the Pyrenees in 1659, it has remained Spanish, and looks it.

Even at nearly 4,000 feet it can be hot in Puigcerdá at high

noon, but the heat is made tolerable by the peaceful and un-
ceasing sound of running streams, ice cold from the surrounding peaks, and filled with the most delicious speckled trout,
and at night, even in summer, there are sudden inexplicable
cool gusts that test the heavy stones placed on the roof tiles to
help keep them in place. For those who are incurably active
there is an excellent 18-hole golf course a little way up the
valley, ministered to by the luxurious Hotel del Golf together
with its own swimming-pool.

With some of the highest peaks to our right there is a lovely
summer road running from Puigcerdá for 45 miles due west
beside the River Segre, passing tiny Romanesque chapels and
mediaeval castles, to bring us to the unimaginably ancient-
seeming town of Seo de Urgel, the gateway to Andorra. When
first I saw it it was, quite literally, the only gateway into that
tiny feudal principality, though early in the 1930s the French
opened another way out to the north by the nearly 8,000-feet
high pass known as La Porte d'Envalira which is, however,
regularly snowed up each winter.

There is always something attractive about a minuscule state
surviving into these prosaic times – Monaco, San Marino,
Liechtenstein, Sikkim, Andorra – I have tried them all – but I
find that I prefer my mountains at a greater distance. In
Andorra 'dawn' often occurs at 10 a.m. and 'sunset' around
3.30 p.m., when the sun is obstructed by the peaks on the
opposite side of your narrow ravine of a valley.

Even so you should drive through it if the occasion offers
(and you are a good driver) as it is the last survivor of the once
quite numerous independent 'neutral states' of the Pyrenean
valleys, and its co-rulers are the President of France and the
Bishop of Urgel.

Andorra has never had an official war or revolution, but
there was believed to have been quite serious trouble there in
the mid-1930s, when a journalist friend of mine was rushed
from Fleet Street to find out just what the trouble was. Was it
Communist or Fascist, were the bloated capitalists being
beastly to the downtrodden workers – or what? He spent a
week there, but was baffled by the fact that whenever he made
enquiries his informant would always begin by telling him – in

Catalan and detail – all about a thirteenth-century law to do with cattle grazing rights which, my friend justifiably felt, would be even more incomprehensible to his readers, if any, than it was to him. Urged on by irritable cables from his Editor he delved still deeper into the matter, and finally discovered that the Council of Twenty were gravely displeased by the French 'Viguier's' appointment of a non-Spanish Syndic-General. Totally baffled, he resigned and took heavily to drink. In fact, the population of about 8,000 are wholly dedicated to smuggling, growing bad tobacco to fill cigarettes to go into the forged packs of well-known British and American brands, or, failing all else, to trying to steal one another's cattle – but it is all rather good fun if you are, like myself, a short-term escapist.

Seo de Urgel, which I find enchanting, was founded in 820, and although it has only a few thousand inhabitants, possesses a cathedral, dedicated to St Odo, so enormous that it could comfortably accommodate every single one of them all at once. It was built by Maestro Ramon, a Lombard, but has been battered and weathered until tall grasses sprout like a grizzled beard from between its crumbling stones. I have seen many far older buildings, but the Cathedral of Seo de Urgel always looks to me by far the tiredest of them all. The nearby eleventh-century San Miguel still lifts its towers to pray, but the cathedral seems to me to be sinking back, gratefully, into the earth from which it sprang when the Faith was still young.

2. The Mountain Valleys of the Pyrenees

As happens too often when following the Pyrenees from the sadly polluted blue of the Mediterranean to the still clean waters of the Cantabrican Sea, the mountains at Seo de Urgel close in around us, and force us to run south. In this case it is beside the River Segre, but it is a pleasant valley, with red-brown, stone-built villages pressing into sunny corners against the winds of winter, of small, green fields filled with fat cattle, of bright mountain flowers lit with the delicate green or golden flame of slender poplars, of lawn-like meadows studded with autumn crocus, and orchards glowing with brightly coloured, ripening fruit.

Theoretically we should continue all the way to Lerida, Cataluña's second city but, despite a history going back to the time when it was held for Pompey by Africanus, Lerida, for me, died during the days when it was torn apart by an Anarchist mob in 1936 and, somehow, has never come to life again. Fortunately, if you do not mind a quite short spell of poor road, there is a way to 'cut the corner' south of Artesa de Segre, crossing the river to Belaguer – in both there are fine twelfth- and thirteenth-century churches – which brings you into the next north–south valley; that of the River Noguera Pallaresa.

It is tempting to follow the railway north to Tremp, and beyond into the mountain and lake district which provides most of Barcelona's hydro-electric power. I followed it once (and both the road and railway struggle on still farther) past peaks rising to well over 9,000 feet, but I would not advise it, unless you are trying to prove something or to win a medal. It is better to cross to Balaguer and continue west to the motor road at Alfarras, and then to keep going determinedly until you reach the peace and comfort of the Government-operated *parador* at Viella in the Vale of Aran.

Opposite you – but not too close as in Andorra – is Mount Aneto, the highest of all the Pyrenean peaks – and the sinister-sounding Montes Maldetas. At your feet is the confluence of the Rivers Garonne and Negro, and you are again not very far from the frontier with France. Even so, it was not until 1925 that you could cross it by other means than upon your own feet by a rough bridle path, assisted by a very tough mountain pony.

Until the beginning of last century the Vale of Aran was virtually independent; it was annexed to France by Napoleon in 1808, but it was finally recognised as Spanish by the Congress of Vienna in 1815.

Like most small Pyrenean towns and villages Viella looks battered by storm and time, solidly built of strong stone, and hiding for protection in each fold and corner that the land can provide.

You drive through a long tunnel under a shoulder of 9,000-feet Mount Biciberri just before reaching Viella, which itself is well over 3,000 feet up, crouching around its massive old church and, by this time, you may well be beginning to wonder just what to expect next. What does happen is an abrupt emergence into the almost sophisticated elegance of the state-operated parador.

There is a concession to Pyrenean custom in the form of a circular building with a fireplace (and so a chimney) but set in the centre, which is obviously a sound idea since more people can sit round it than the conventional half-circle permits. The smoke drifts into the bell-shaped roof and escapes through a normal-sized opening. If it works in these high places, where for eight months of the year the gusts from the snow-covered peaks cannot be ignored, then it would certainly work anywhere but, except for the Pyrenees – and in a Tartar 'yurt' – I have seen it nowhere else. However, here in Viella it is for the

5   *This bridge, built by the Romans near Jaca (Huesca) is
     still in use today, though not for motor traffic*

public rooms only, which stand apart, beside the swimming-pool, while the bedrooms are of an entirely modern design, facing south towards the sun.

This is a good place to be if you are in search of somewhere in which to be at peace for a short while. The Vale of Aran is a place of lakes and mountains, and air that has never even heard of pollution. From the parador you look down a smiling valley of green-shadowed hills, and live in a state of undemanding physical comfort – but I realise that few people share my pleasure, short-lived I agree (though powerful while it lasts), in doing absolutely nothing in a perfect setting!

This is what would, in earlier times, have been called 'perfect walking country', but if you do not mind driving slowly over country tracks, almost all of the places I visited long ago on foot can today be reached by car.

An obvious visit is only three miles west to Artiés, where there is a mountain chalet-refuge belonging to the Viella parador, and it is from there that the hearty ones gather for explorations into the great mountain massif to the south, including the hidden mountain lakes of San Maurcio and Estangento, high on the shoulders of 9,360-feet Mount Montseny. There are large trout in these lakes, but so inbred that their heads are larger than their bodies, so that they make poor and bone-fraught eating. (You will do better, if you want a trout-eating orgy, to visit the Hosteria de Don Gaspar de Portola.) There, too, you may catch sight of the rare *capra hispanica* – though there are many more in the Gredos Mountains near Avila, where they may be shot. Theoretically there are also brown bear around, but they are almost extinct in the Pyrenees, though still fairly plentiful in Asturias, between 'Leon and Oviedo.

Here, in the Vale of Aran the tiny town of Salardú, a stroll only from the refuge, is still impressively surrounded by its fortified ramparts, and there is a mediaeval castle set decoratively upon a little promontory between the rivers Garonne and Inola. I can find no trace of it having been involved in a battle or a siege, but the place obviously took itself very seriously six or seven hundred years ago, and there are some solid-looking sixteenth-century houses, such as the fortified

6 *Hermitage of Our Lady of Gabanas, Alcala de Ebro*

Casa de Berentete, and the fourteenth-century fortified Casa de Bastete at Unyá, less than a mile away.

The thirteenth-century church at Salardú also came as rather a surprise to me in such a remote place, but its Romanesque 'Cristo de Salardú' is, I later learned, well known to the experts, and much has been written about it. In short, this corner of the Vale is a rewarding place for those with the time and the taste for such unspectacular discoveries.

It is only ten miles from our comfortable parador to the Puerto de Bonaigua, though in this distance you will have climbed a further 3,650 feet. Once there, at 6,800 feet, you will have reached the watershed of the Pyrenees, and the country around you is almost completely unpopulated – wild, but very beautiful in season – and the end of the world from early November until May. Perhaps you may find it a little frightening if you are alone and unused to such tremendous solitude and, anyway, it is something of a relief to finish with the corniche-type road down to Esterri de Aneu.

But it would be merely repetitious to enlarge here in detail upon the many battered little Romanesque churches of the area, some of them, such as that of Tredos, going back to the twelfth century, and earlier. They are small and brown and very very old, and the bas reliefs to be seen in them tell of a strange world of simple faith, complete with monsters, devils, saints and witches, in the intimate language that became lost or unrecognisable in the later, loftier greatness of Gothic. It is a strange, dark little world of its own, now found only in places which may inspire either love or boredom in the individual, but a world which one may sense more easily than describe.

Now we must leave Cataluña for Aragón, and from Viella we have no choice but to turn south, and the wise will keep on going south all the way until the road turns west through Benabarre, and from Barbastro to Huesca. There are exciting mountain roads turning off from Pont de Suert, Castellon de Sos and Ainsa which would bring us to our next real destination in the National Park of Ordesa, but, if you take them, you will be completely off the map among peaks rising to well over 9,000 feet and, should you have a breakdown, the sole relief you can count on would be from the daily bus which might, just possibly, be having a day off! However, *en passant*, there is a practicable summer road from Pont de Suert to the increasingly popular winter-sports resort of Benasque to the west of Mount Aneto, but it is rather too spartan for me.

Our west-running road passes through Graus, a pleasant little place with a fifteenth-century arcaded plaza and a tiny Romanesque Church of San Miguel and, if you are so minded, a dramatically situated sixteenth-century hermitage just to the southwest.

Barbastro is an ancient city – though the word 'city' may seem rather grand for a place of less than 10,000 inhabitants. It was destroyed, not built, 2,000 years ago by Pompey, and named Brutina (rather offensively one feels) by Decius Brutus. Then it disappears from history for a millennium when it was conquered by the Moors in 1065, and later sacked by a Norman army allied to the Catalans. When the worst of the Moslem invasion and the mindless fury of the Dark Ages had at last drowned themselves in blood, the people of the town began work on the cathedral, which, however, was not finished until 1533, following plans drawn by Juan de Segura. Seen from outside, the west front is the most attractive, and the whole is topped by a six-sided tower and fan-type vaults. Internally the most striking features are the choir stalls of Navarrese oak, carried out between 1582 and 1604. Only a few miles away is the Convent of Sigeña built by Alfonso II and Queen Sancha in 1188, but its exquisite Mudejar Chapel was destroyed, together with some irreplaceable thirteenth-century wall paintings, by Republican forces during the Civil War.

Huesca is only some 1,500 feet above sea level – the lowest that we have been for quite a long time – on the most southern outpost of the Pyrenees. South the land falls away gently to Zaragoza – or Saragossa, if you prefer it – beside Spain's greatest river, the Ebro.

My first view of Huesca was late in 1936 from a neighbouring hilltop, where I parked the borrowed motorcycle which had brought me from Barcelona to try to discover 'the front'. I had required a number of passes from various trigger-happy types before I could leave, and each one was marked by a distinctive rubber stamp. I soon realised why, when I observed that, more often than not, my 'movement order' was scrutinised upside-down. Few of the guards could read, but all had committed to memory the special stamp of the F.A.I. (Anarchists), U.G.T. (Workers' Union) and the P.O.U.M. (Trotskyists), and they were enough for the moment, though they were to be bloodily at war with one another by the following spring.

Sitting on my hilltop overlooking the fortress town and, indigestibly, munching a rather stale loaf of bread, garnished with the contents of a tin of sardines, swallowed only with the assistance of some raw, but heartening red wine (such luxuries were soon to disappear) I experienced that rather odd sensation of being on both sides of an invisible line. It was a quiet day, and what breeze there was carried clearly the sounds of a car hooting and, above all of church bells – a sound which I had not heard for months in Barcelona – another world, as near, yet as remote, as one peopled by the dead.

I was to learn a little later that not so far away, in Lerida, Durruti was dealing with his own particular military problem by methods of which I was soon to be a sickened witness.

At the outbreak of the Civil War in July, thousands of women accompanied their menfolk to 'the front', and since all officers, or even discipline as we know it, had been abolished, this army of camp followers could not be stopped. In brief: without their girlfriends the men would not move. Inevitably the *milicianas*, as they called themselves, caused fatal fights for ownership among the men and, in a matter of months, half the male fighting force was incapacitated with venereal disease – and this was before the days of antibiotics.

Durruti knew that he could never separate them by any orders he, or the Catalan Government, might give, so he commandeered all the lorries he could lay hands on, and let it be known that these were going first to withdraw the *milicianas* to a 'leave centre' well behind the lines, then to bring up reinforcements of *milicianos* who, he said, were ready and waiting to take over the fight, and, finally, transport the present frontliners to rejoin their girlfriends in Lerida.

He succeeded in persuading several hundred of the women to accept the idea, with the permission of their menfolk. When he got the lorry loads of cheering young women some twenty miles away from the front they were turned out on to the roadside, and machine-gunned to death. When I passed the following day 400 bodies were being buried in the shallow roadside ditches – but most of the men at the front gradually regained their capacity to fight. From what he himself told me Durruti, who a few months later was shot in the back in what the world was told was an inter-anarcho-syndicalist fight, was personally quite certain that he would die as an act of vengeance from one of the men or women whom he had separated here, just outside Huesca – but he died content that his ghastly crime postponed defeat for his side a little longer than would otherwise have been the case.

I always thought of Durruti as a second Marat – unquestionably a monster, perhaps even insane, but completely sincere in his beliefs.

Since Huesca was never captured – though its surroundings were badly damaged – it is still alive today despite its great age, and still a dignified Aragonese city-fortress.

Huesca was chosen by the renegade Roman General Quintus Sertorius to be his capital and permanent military headquarters against the followers of Sulla, and he even established a university there as early as 75 B.C. – which makes Oxbridge look positively 'red brick' by comparison – but only three years later he was assassinated. The little city was swallowed up in one of the first of the overwhelming Moslem waves of conquest, waves which were only going to break at Poitiers in France and in corners of Asturias in northern Spain, and it was not finally liberated until the arrival of Pedro I in 1096. The Christian capital was then shifted there from Jaca until the Kingdom of Aragón established itself, after a five years' siege, in Zaragoza in 1118.

Huesca's oldest church is San Pedro el Viejo, begun in its present form in 1134, its predecessor having been permitted as a place of Christian worship by the enlightened Moors during the entire period of their occupation. It is a very holy place as it contains the bones of Saints Justus and Pastor, and there is a rugged beauty in the 'Romanesque' carved capitals in its cloister.

(I asked an American-speaking Spanish companion who Saints

Justus and Pastor were, and he replied, rather engagingly I thought, 'Sorry, but I'm not too hot on my hagiology'!)

Naturally the late Gothic cathedral dominates the sky line and, if you climb to the top of its octagonal tower, there is a breath-taking view; in one direction of the Pyrenees in all their glory and, in the other, of the fertile valley of the Ebro – that is if you have any breath to be taken after climbing so many steep stone steps.

But there is much else to see in this pleasant old ochre and white-coloured city, not the least being the sixteenth-century silver panels depicting the Seven Joys of Mary, and the university – that same pre-Christian university founded by Sertorius, though refounded – after a little interlude of 1,400 years or so – by Pedro IV.

To be honest, the road north from Huesca via Sabiñánigo, Briescas and Torla to the parador in the National Park of Ordesa is not one about which I would expect the RAC to enthuse, but the distances involved are not great if you think yourself out of our rat-race 70 m.p.h. motorway mentality, and settle for a relaxing 40 or so. Be satisfied with the certainty that you are on your way to one of the loveliest of all Spanish Pyrenean mountain valleys. You may not realise this when you first see the parador itself, which is unremarkable, but you will if, after confirming your accommodation, you continue for another couple of miles or so, with the rock-strewn river on your right – rocks, incidentally, of a size bearing witness to its power and fury after the melting of the first snows – when you will suddenly come to the end of the road with, beyond it, an open, green glade, the floor of which, when first I saw it, was thickly strewn with delicious mushrooms.

Already well over 4,000 feet, this is the starting or arrival point for the climb to the once famous Cirque de Gavarnie and other semi-professional ascents, such as that to the 'Brèche de Roland', a pass at over 9,200 feet (through which the legendary hero hewed a 350-feet deep cleft with his sword Durandel), or to 11,000-feet high Monte Perdido, and many others, most of them demanding the services of a professional guide, and a considerable amount of previous mountaineering experience.

The Vale as I first saw it was a place of silent enchantment.

The poplars were tall candle flames burning before some invisible altar, and the silence so complete that it sang. The only habitation was a rather ramshackle, dark brown house, from the sole chimney of which some very white smoke rose completely straight into the cool, still air. At the other side of the mushroom-dappled, very green lawn a fawn was placidly drinking from a shallow pool, and merely pricked her ears at me briefly before deciding that I was harmless. Being a Tolkien fan I half expected that the door of the little house would open, and Gandalf in person emerge.

The truth, more prosaic, revealed that the house was for storing mountaineering gear of all kinds, but on its wooden door were incised the names and dates of those who had successfully made the climb from France, some of them dating back to the 1880s, most of them English, and all, I suppose, long dead.

When you have had your fill of Ordesa – and I admit that if I could afford it, only winter would drive me away – we must retrace our way for the comparatively few miles through Torla, Briescas and Sabiñánigo if we are to come to Jaca. But although the road is poor there are continual consolations along the way. To reach the parador of Ordesa you may not have taken much note of smoke-blackened Torla, yet its thirteenth-century church contains a magnificent processional cross which you may see *if* you can get someone to find the man who keeps the key! If that takes a while – and well it may – you can gaze to your heart's content at the spectacular backdrop of mountains, in which you may glimpse a distant herd of wild horses still living as God intended – free as the wind.

There is something reassuring about the defensive walls of Jaca set above the chattering river Aragón. It is a small, snug place of barely 10,000 inhabitants, but justifiably proud of the part it played as the first real headquarters for the reconquest of the ancient kingdom. Here you are still nearly 2,700 feet above the lovely, polluted Mediterranean, and surrounded by a history that goes back well over 2,000 years.

It was captured by Porcius Cato in 194 B.C., and fragments of the ramparts he then built may still be recognised, though they are topped with the turreted walls of a later date. It was overrun by the Moors in A.D. 716, but quickly recaptured in 760 – quickly that is in terms of Spain's 800-year crusade for liberation. A ferocious counter-attack was only just beaten off in 795, the women – as in Zaragoza – playing an heroic part.

(It seems that Aragonese women are definitely not to be trifled with: perhaps fortunately, it is one of the few areas of Spain which only rarely produces attractive ones!)

Jaca's massive cathedral was founded in 814, but the present building dates from 1063, when Norman William was plotting his descent upon our own coasts, and in her silver shrine are the remains of St Orosia whose feast days are from June 25th–30th. You may be curious to see the *Libro de la Cadena* – a chained thirteenth-century volume listing the city's ancient privileges and rights, but there are many other noble buildings in Jaca if you are in the mood to browse into its byways.

Every road from Jaca contains a promise. To the north you see the vast panorama of the Pyrenees, leading to one of the six historical passes through them. This of Somport, or Cadanchu, was the invasion route of the Romans, Goths and Vandals and was later also used by pilgrims on their way to Santiago from Italy and Central Europe.

Eleanor of Poitou, sister of our Richard Coeur de Lion, entered Spain by the Somport Pass to marry Alfonso VIII, accompanied by five Spanish bishops and a company of Cistercian and Benedictine monks, and dubbed it 'Portibus Asperi'. She and her retinue stayed in the Priory Hospital of Santa Cristina de Somport, today only a pile of stones – she would have been better off at the neighbouring spa of Panticosa, with its four hot thermal springs!

We have just come from the northeast in Ordesa, south of us lies Mount Oroel, while west the road follows the river to the ancient monasteries which, in the early years of the Reconquest, were the head, heart and soul of embattled Christian Spain.

It is only a three-hour ascent on foot from Jaca to the summit, and is a popular *romaria* – that peculiarly Spanish mixture of a picnic outing and a pilgrimage to a holy place. There is the huge cave, where in 724 300 Christian knights met to swear that they would create the Kingdom of Aragón, today sanctified as the Chapel of the Virgin of the Cave.

Far more interesting is to drive south to the village of Bernués, 11 miles from Jaca, and then take a mountain track for the remaining seven miles to the Monastery de San Juan de la Peña.

Originally a modest hermitage it ultimately had control over 65 monasteries and 126 churches. It contained the Council Chamber of King Alfonso I (the Embattled), and it was from here that he set out to liberate Zaragoza. It was often the home of King Ramiro I and his immediate successors, and is the pantheon of the Aragonese kings.

It is a strange place, even for Spain. It really consists of two churches in one. The lower, a kind of crypt, was built on the site of a Hermitage in the ninth century, sheltering under a great cliff near the deserted town of Pano by King Sancho Garces I in 905–25, and shows strong Latino-Byzantine influences. Twenty-six steps lead to the atrium, with the same number of carved tombs of kings, heroes and abbots, set in two rows of niches – the most complete Romanesque pantheon in existence. A horse-shoe shaped door with Mozarabic lettering leads into the ruined cloisters, which are roofed by the living rock of the mountainside.

The second, thirteenth-century, church-pantheon is richly carved with stories from Genesis, the Temptation, and of Adam ploughing with two horses while Eve spins. Here Cain slays Abel and adjacent capitals depict New Testament themes. While naïve in execution the whole building has an unmistakable sense of ceremonial dignity.

Naturally such a place has been sacked and burned more than once – Napoleon's Marshal Suchet in 1809 being the last offender – but it still speaks clearly of the days when the Moors were always threatening, and it has a complete fortified wall, for these were the times when a bishop would throw off his mitre and priestly vestments to reveal a suit of mail, and personally take a whack at the raiders with a 20-pound spiked mace – swords, it seems, were frowned upon as being unsuitable for prelates!

Incidentally, it was in the Monastery of San Juan de la Peña that the first Latin Mass was performed in Spain – in 1071, by a special Legate sent for the purpose by Pope Alexander II. The Christianised Gothic kings of Spain, overthrown by the Moors early in the eighth century, used the Visigothic liturgy, which may still be heard on special rare occasions in Toledo.

If you are monastery-minded, it is only a few miles from Jaca to the ruined Convent of Santa Cruz de la Serós, endowed in the tenth century, of which the octagonal cupola still stands. Above the door is written 'I am the door of good fortune: pass through me ye faithful'. It is Romanesque at its best, but there is little more to see and, should it be a question of choice, then choose San Juan de la Peña every time.

But being near to so big a city as Zaragoza there may be a temptation to abandon the High Places for a while – though it means retracing our way through Huesca – but, as no doubt Oscar Wilde said, the great thing about temptation is never to resist it. To date we have followed the almost unchanged byways of an older Spain (where the voice of the packaged tourist is emphatically *not* heard in the land) and in Zaragoza we shall be plunging into what is at least a major stopping place in the current of that Brave New Spain which is doing its best to lose its Spanishness.

('Spanishness', or *Hispanidad*, is quite a genuine cult in Spain, devised to bind the mother country to her former colonies in Spanish America. So generally acknowledged is it that there is a well-worn chestnut on the subject still occasionally in circulation. In this an American millionaire commissions the most prominent British, French, German and Spanish authors that money can buy to produce a definitive work upon elephants. The Englishman produces a slim volume, profusely illustrated, entitled, *My Good Friend the Elephant, and How Best to Kill him*; the German, three heavy tomes entitled, *The Elephant: Does He Exist?*; the Frenchman, a tasteful work named, *La Vie Amoureux d'Eléfant. Montrant Les Sept Nouveaux Poses*, and the Spaniard a vague but highly literary volume entitled *Elefantidad*.)

But there is a special reason why we should, at least briefly, visit Zaragoza, for it is here that a link may be forged in the long chain of our pilgrimage to Santiago de Compostela.

According to the Golden Legend, St James the Apostle – 'Santiago' in Spanish – elder son of Zeberde and Salome, and brother of St John the Evangelist, spent the years that followed the Crucifixion preaching in Jewry, Samaria and Spain, arriving by sea at Iria, now Padrón, in Spanish Galicia, and then making his way through Coimbra and Braga in what today is Portugal (where he made Pedro Rates a Bishop) and continuing east until he came to the city on the Ebro known as Caesar Augusta, or Zaragoza, in the year 40.

The Saint had reached a crisis of frustration, such as occasionally afflicts men of great spirituality but, on the night of his arrival he was wakened by the fair voices of angels singing the 'Ave Maria', and the walls of his poor room seemed to vanish. Then Our Lady appeared, seated upon a throne, carrying a small image of herself, set upon a pillar of jasper, and indicated the exact spot upon which her greatest temple was to be built.

Today the small Virgin del Pilar is one of the most revered in all Spain, and the interior of the basilica which houses it, with its multi-coloured cupolas, is like some vast, underground city.

The modest chapel built at the orders of the Apostle – and Zaragoza was one of the first places in Spain to become Christian – was replaced by a church in the thirteenth century, but this was destroyed by fire, and what you see today is mostly eighteenth century – modern by Spanish standards.

Strengthened, and infinitely encouraged by his vision, St James named his disciple Athenasius to be Zaragoza's first Bishop and, after ordaining his friend Theodore as a priest, straightly charged him to await his return, after his necessary martyrdom in the Holy Land, at the same little Galician port of Iria where he had first set foot in Spain to begin his ministry there.

Perhaps it is as well to finish this part of the Golden Legend now, before returning to the twentieth century. This tells us that the martyred Apostle's body was duly transported back to Spain in seven days, in a ship without sails, rudder or crew, and that Theodore was there to meet it. With the help of his own converts he reverently lifted the body from the magical ship, and laid it upon a great stone, which received it within itself as though it were made of soft wax instead of hardest granite, and the body was left there upon the shore, safely sealed, but visible, within the great stone.

Something of these events had been reported to Queen Lupa of Galicia, who promptly arrested Theodore and his followers, and sent them to the King of Spain who, in turn, imprisoned them. However, that same night, they were released by an angel. Infuriated, the King sent a company of his knights to bring them back, but a bridge they were crossing collapsed, and the King, discerning divine intervention, was converted, sending Queen Lupa a message to say that they were to be helped in every possible way.

However, the female of the species, living up to repute, gave orders that they should 'take her oxen and bring the Saint's body to her', though knowing full well that 'her oxen' were the ferocious *toros de lidia*, or fighting bulls,* and would certainly kill Theodore and his followers on sight. The bulls, on the contrary, immediately recognised the sacred nature of their task and, abandoning their normal ferocity, carried out the humble work of dragging their burden to Queen Lupa as though they were indeed no more than oxen. This incredible spectacle finally convinced her, and she presented Theodore with the Pico Sacro – the Holy Peak – for use as a mausoleum, and herself paid for an altar to be built over the tomb.

There the Apostle at last found rest, and no more is heard of him for some eight centuries. I will leave the story of what happened when he emerged from his sleep in the guise of Santiago Matamoros (Slayer of Moors) until we are nearer to having earned the scallop shell which, for many centuries, was the proud possession only of those who had completed their pilgrimage along the Road to Santiago.†

Zaragoza has never been one of my favourite Spanish cities (perhaps partly because the first time I saw it I was under open arrest, following the fall of Barcelona, on my way to Burgos early in February 1939) though I once spent some time pleasantly there in the 1950s doing research work for a film 'treat-

---

* Fighting bulls simply cannot be excluded from any Spanish legend however ancient it may be, or however pious it's intent! c.s.

† See Professor Walter Starkie's masterly, *The Road to Santiago*, published by John Murray.

ment' on the life of Goya. The village of his birth is only a few miles away, and some of his earliest work is to be seen in the Basilica de Nuestra Señora del Pilar. Incidentally, it was to escape the pressing attentions of the Holy Inquisition in Zaragoza that Goya left, distinctly hurriedly, to find immortal fame in Madrid as court painter to Carlos IV, Joseph Bonaparte and the lamentable Ferdinand VII. The Holy Office was getting more than a little peeved with Goya's rendering of all priests as wearing the long, furry ears of donkeys!

Zaragoza is Spain's Sandhurst, but it took me some time to reconcile the militancy of the splendidly uniformed cadets with their habitual public appearance licking interminably at jumbo-sized ice-cream cones! But do not be deceived by this into thinking that they are not every bit as tough, or tougher, than their British counterparts. It is just that among the Spanish it is not, as with us, considered a sign of 'manliness' to get drunk, for the simple reason that alcohol is plentiful and cheap, and they drink wine (though perhaps slightly watered, like the ancient Greeks) as soon as they are off mother's milk. Additionally, there are no roars of 'Time, Gentlemen, please' (or, more recently, I note with regret, of 'Everybody Out!') to lead to the fatal last minute business of trying to beat the clock. Café-Bars, or, more recently, 'Whiskerias', are open more or less all day and night and, as a result, you will see very little drunkenness in Spain except in Andalucia – where it is almost universal! I am sure that if pubs were always open in Britain there would be a sharp decline in both drunkenness and the crimes of violence that so often stem from it, but the British Non-Conformist Conscience will defend the existing niggling and ineffectual restrictions at any price, as they will continue to try to equate 'drink' with 'sin'! They are pained when you point out that the Bible specifically states that God 'gave wine to make glad the heart of Man', or remind them of the nature of Christ's first recorded miracle – but it is a shame to deprive them of what is probably their only hope of feeling 'better' than their fellow men.

Zaragoza has the historic reputation of having withstood sieges longer than almost any city since Priam's Troy.

First, having invited the help of Charlemagne against the

Saracens, when he arrived from Paderborn in 778, he had to fight to get in, and some believe that the Aragonese were not entirely innocent of the attack upon him when he was retreating through the Roncesvalles Pass in the Pyrenees. Then the city's Moorish overlords withstood the siege of Alfonso (The Embattled) from 1115 until 1118. Nearly 700 years later Napoleon's General Lefebvre encountered a fanatical resistance when he tried to take the city in June 1808, and even when the invaders were reinforced by 30,000 fresh troops under Lannes, Mortier and Junot, the city would not surrender despite fire and plague. Byron's 'Maid of Saragossa' immortalised the part played by a woman, handling guns and hurling roof tiles upon the invaders. Only after a house-to-house assault through the smoking ruins did the French finally succeed in reducing the place in February 1809.

Yet again the people of Zaragoza resisted a surprise attack by the Carlist leader Cabañero, whom they captured in a church and made prisoner in 1838. Lastly, firmly in the hands of the Nationalists at the outbreak of the Civil War, the Anarcho-Syndicalists never looked like succeeding where Napoleon's generals had so nearly failed.

Perhaps because of all these historic sieges Zaragoza does not strike the casual visitor of today as a remarkably old city – at least not by Spanish standards – but there are large numbers of seventeenth-century palaces down many hidden side-streets if you have the time and inclination to stroll away from the commercial centres.

There is not, therefore, much that can compete with the cathedral if you are in search of antiquity. In Christianised Visigoth days there was a church on the same site, which the Berbers* replaced with a mosque in the eighth century. The mosque was reconstructed as a church in 1119, being modified in the thirteenth century after it had become the see for a archbishopric in 1318. Mozarabic, Mudejar, Romanesque, Renaissance Gothic and Plateresque additions can be discerned

---

* Berbers, Saracens, Moors and Egyptians were all in the Moslem horde that overran so much of western Europe in the century following the prophet's death: it was purely fortuitous that Zaragoza's conquerors were Saracens and Berbers. c.s.

even by the more or less inexpert eye but, strangely enough, this tremendous collection of different styles has achieved aesthetic harmony. The whole is unimaginable anywhere else but Spain, but the overall effect is tremendously impressive.

The nearly square mosque plan is apparent in the slender pillars, though Christian hands must have sculpted the capitals with figures of children. If you are interested in such things, you will find a black stone to the left of the high altar which marks the burial place of the heart of Don Balthasar Carlos, son of Philip IV, the Infante who appears so often in the paintings of Velázques, who died in Zaragoza of smallpox in 1646.

In the Sacristy there are some 400-years-old priestly vestments – exquisitely painted cobwebs – still, on very rare occasions, in use. Here, too, are many canvases by Goya, Ribera and Zurbarán. These last two artists seem to have caught the eye of the great collectors only comparatively recently, though always valued by the Spaniards themselves even higher than Goya, whose occasional stark horror still vaguely shocks them.

Of other places, Zaragoza's university is rather overshadowed by the Military Academy, training place of Franco's designated successor. More rewarding are the ancient byways of the suburb known as Torrero, and the sixteenth-century Carthusian Monastery of Aula Dei, with its 11 Goya murals.

West and northwest of Zaragoza lie the worthy but, to me, not very exciting cities of Soria, visited by those to whom shards of polychrome pottery from the Celto-Iberian capital of Numantia may be a source of interest, and Logroño, where we will later call to pay our respects to the best table wines grown in Spain.

Soria – except for one unusually beautiful Romanesque façade belonging to twelfth-century Santo Domingo – is little but the museum from an archaeologists' dig on the site of Numancia, which withstood Scipio Africanus the Younger for a year, from 134 to 133 B.C., and paid with its utter destruction for its obstinacy, an obstinacy which included the eating of its own dead rather than surrender. Its only other claim to distinction is the unenviable one of, year after year, registering the lowest minimum temperatures of any Spanish provincial capital.

Ruins often have a living tale to tell: Numancia, and therefore Soria, is for those of whom, alas, I am not one, particularly when I am in a land so lovely and living as Spain, to
whom fragments have a reality. Besides, we still have a little
unfinished business in that strange world of the early Reconquest. Only then shall we be free to reach the green waters of
the Cantabrican Sea, the Basques and, finally, the direct road
westwards to Santiago.

7   *Jaca (Huesca): Monastery of Santa Cruz de la Seros. When
the Christians were forced back to the Pyrenees, monasteries
were built with an eye to defence against Moorish raids*

3. The Ancient Kingdoms of Aragon and Navarre

Almost everyone has their own private mental picture of a castle in Spain. This was typified for many in the much publicised Alcazar of Segovia which appeared, presumably transferred to Wales or North Devon by Merlin, for use as a backdrop to King Arthur in the shockingly bad Harris–Redgrave musical called 'Camelot'.

For many years it was close to my own ideal, but latterly I have had to find somewhere that has not yet been subjected to film treatment and, on this, my latest visit, I found an alternative, which I share with few but eagles, in this early Reconquest part of Spain. Fortunately it is not too easy to reach, so it may last my time. A little way off the Huesca–Sabiñanigo road you will find the almost unbelievable eleventh-century Royal Castle of Loarre, with its mighty, bastioned walls enclosing no less than two thirteenth-century churches, both with marvellously sculptured capitals.

It is well off the beaten track, and has few two-legged visitors. Built into the living rock, it towers up to a great battlemented look-out turret, a place which once seen must capture the imagination for ever. Standing at this immense height you can hear nothing but the wind moving across the short grass, and the infinitely remote cry of a rare hunting eagle. It gazes across a seemingly uninhabited grey-green and golden-brown world to the small lake of Sotonera.

You will find little written about it, but if you want to recapture for a moment the great, half-forgotten dream of the

8 *Daroca, Zaragoza, much as it was when Goya was born nearby*

Reconquest, you will learn more about it in half an hour there than you will in any library.

Running northwest from Zaragoza I had to be unusually strong-minded, in order not to turn off to Borja, whose castle was the home of the Borgias, more particularly as I had always associated the wicked Pope Alexander VI, and his fascinatingly infamous son and daughter Cesare and Lucrezia, with the highly decorative Castle of Jativa, near Valencia. It seems that I was wrong, and that they moved to Jativa only in the fourteenth century. I was also passing by the Abbey of Veruela, dating from the twelfth century, which makes it one of the oldest Cistercian monasteries in Spain, now a Jesuit college, but in Spain there is always so much to see that you simply dare not allow yourself to wander from the general lines of your intended route. It would be pleasant, but I know from experience that it is almost always fatal, unless all considerations of both time and money have been eliminated from your life!

Instead I therefore virtuously crossed the Ebro and, passing through Egea de los Caballeros, came to the Castle of Sábada and Sos del Rey Catolico, whose Palacio Sada was the birthplace of that rather unattractive (and very Aragonese) Ferdinand who, by his marriage to Isabella of Castile, was to unite Spain, and then to drive the Moors from their last strongholds of Malaga, Granada and Tarifa during the last decade of the fifteenth century.

Sos del Rey Catolico is an ancient walled town – walls which today protect only a very few thousand people – but it contains the impressive Church of San Esteban, and much else of beauty and great age. But we are now close to our immediate objective of Sangüesa, Tesa and the once great Monastery of de Leyre, which marks our arrival upon the true Pilgrim's Way.

You may notice the sudden disappearance of the Aragonese *baturro* patois, a language barrier brought about by the physical crossing of an invisible line which, anyway, ceased to exist, even on paper, when, centuries ago, the kingdoms of Aragon and Navarre became parts of united Spain – but the change is far less of a shock than will be produced by our first encounter with the jaw-cracking language of the Basques after leaving Pamplona.

Almost equally great changes are discernible between dances and costumes of almost any two parallel valleys separated, as the crow flies, by only 20 or 30 miles – though, admittedly, miles of unscaleable mountain. Where distances are greater this becomes even more obvious, and the war-like *jota* of Aragon is profoundly different to the statuesque *jota* of Segovia, or the almost languorous Mediterranean *jota* of Valencia. Here, in the Aragónese mountains, it is a dance displaying an almost alarming concentration of total fury!

It is sad that the slightly absurd, internal dynastic Carlist Wars should have been the cause of the destruction in 1835 of the thousand years old Cistercian Monastery of de Leyre. St Eulogius lived here for a while in 851–2, and it became a powerful centre of Cluniac reform in the eleventh century, but its ruin was a consequence of Ferdinand VII's decision to revoke the Salic Law in favour of his nymphomaniac daughter Isabella, rather than allow his brother, Carlos, to succeed him.

It is only a few miles from the ruins of the once great Monastery de Leyre to the eleventh-century pantheon of the Kings of Navarre at Yesa, which overlooks a limpidly clear lake. The many tombs in the very ancient Monastery of San Salvador have suffered with the passing of nearly a millennium, but still possess a certain battered splendour, and the neighbouring Castle of Xavier – sometimes written Javier – birthplace of St Francis Xavier, seems, by comparison, almost modern.

Only five miles away is the really astonishing little town of Sangüesa on the left bank of the River Aragon where, close to the ancient Pilgrim's Bridge, stands Santa Maria la Real, with its beautifully slender octagonal thirteenth-century tower and spire. Even in this land of ancient monasteries and churches, you should pause a while in Sangüesa, for in this same tiny town of less than 4,000 inhabitants, there is also a magnificent embattled, fourteenth-century towered Church of Santiago and, dating from the same century, that of San Salvador. The entire population could be accommodated in any one of the three but, I suppose, in the great days of Faith, there seemed no happier thing to do with wealth and power than to raise yet another place in which to praise the Lord.

Almost more remarkable is the former castle of the Princes

of Viana, now the Town Hall, the fifteenth-century baroque Palace of the Vallesantoro family, and the equally ancient, and almost equally beautiful mansions of the Counts of Guaqui and the Dukes of Granada. For good measure, just outside the town is the Chapel of San Adrian, once the property of the Knights Templar. For such a small place to have so many five-star treasures seems almost incredible – almost an *embarras de richesses*!

But this small place, almost lost on a side road, was once a major gathering place for pilgrims from the eleventh until the fifteenth century. They included Lombards, Irish, Italians, Dutch, Hungarians, British and Byzantines all the way from Turkey, who paused here to recover from their passage over the Pyrenees and where, naturally enough, a great market formed for goods of every kind.

In those times the bell of the Church of Santiago used to toll 40 times at nine, and again at ten every night, to tell lost and benighted pilgrims that they were near this safe place of rest and refreshment. It was rather more than that, with huge, vaulted cellars, which earned it a reprimand for supplying too much wine and not enough bread and meat!

This, today tiny town of barely 4,000 inhabitants, is very well worth a visit, the fourteenth-century wooden image of Santiago, known as the 'Black Santiago' or, in Basque, *Beltza*, is particularly attractive, and the sacristy contains the great silver cross with which the locally born Archbishop of Toledo, Rodrigo Jiminez, led the Christian host in the great Battle of Las Navas de Tolosa in the year 1212, together with an eye-witness account of the battle, and the chains taken from the Christian slaves that were liberated there.

For now we are at last in the mainstream of the Reconquest, and firmly set upon the Pilgrim's Way – even the rough, almost black local wine which is so heartening in these remote and often frozen high places is known as *Vino del Moro* – Moorish wine – because it is unbaptised!

Across the gulf of so many centuries it is not easy to realise the importance attached to the Great Pilgrimage to Compostela except, perhaps, by likening it to that attached to Mecca by Moslems.

But Mecca, Compostela, Rome and even Jerusalem were all surpassed last century by Lourdes, though partly because of the improved communications and decreased dangers of mid-nineteenth-century France. Bernadette died less than a hundred years ago, aged only 35 (incidentally, a chronic asthmatic), and a similar – some cynics say copied – series of revelations were reported by the shepherd girl Lucia, at Fatima in Portugal, which took place as recently as 1917. Lucia in fact, at the moment of writing, still lives in a Closed Order of nuns in Coimbra. These examples strongly suggest that the desire to make a pilgrimage (like the idea of easing one's conscience by sharing the burden of a sin in the confessional) is still something fundamentally rooted in all human nature.

There have been many explanations of this impulse to undertake a pilgrimage. Montaigne's was 'I know what I am fleeing, but not what I am in search of,' but I prefer another: 'I then realised that, as we get older, we become more obsessed by the longing to undertake a hidden journey which will remind us gently of the ultimate one, and evoke for us countless shadowy spirits who, though they have long since been ferried across to the farther bank of the last river, yet continue to haunt us as we plod along the road.'

A cynic once said that the basic motives for the Crusades were mercenary – looting the defeated Infidel was no sin – and in providing a means for escaping from one's wife for a while without a row – and both factors may have been present, though they were emphatically not the primary ones.

Yet all motives were certainly not pure. The gipsies saw the immense possibilities for profitable crime offered by the Pilgrimage. Early in the fifteenth century an enterprising Romany (modestly self-styled the Duke of Little Egypt) secured a peaceful infiltration into a highly xenophobic mediaeval Europe by announcing that he, with 400 of his subjects, was obliged to make the pilgrimage every seven years, because their ancestors had refused help and shelter to Joseph, Mary and the Infant Jesus during the Flight into Egypt from Herod's persecution. He even secured documents of safe conduct from the King of Hungary and, later, from the Pope himself, an exploit still admiringly referred to by the gipsies as the *jojano baro* – the

Great Trick!

The original 400, headed by 'King' Zundle, swelled to a horde by 1438 – and the pickings were rich!

But although the Pilgrimage to Santiago de Compostela was known as the Great Pilgrimage, St James had some severe competition from St Isidor – but first we must return briefly to the Golden Legend.

Christianity had reached its nadir when King Pelayo and his small band of knights issued from the Caves of Covadonga in 718, but by the time of Alfonso II (the Chaste), who reigned from 791 until 842, the Christian forces had become strong enough to extend the original toe-hold along the mountainous coast of Asturias as far west as Galicia.

Then St James Matamoros began to play his part.

A great star, low over a hill, and also little flickering stars* among the bushes which grew upon it, were seen by a hermit and various shepherds who reported the occurrence to Theodomir, Bishop of Iria Flavia, adding that when they approached nearer to investigate, they had heard divinely sweet music. The Bishop accompanied them, and saw and heard the same manifestations. Approaching in deep awe, but unafraid, he began moving the earth aside with his hands and then, with their help, soon came upon an arch covering an altar, beneath which was a sarcophagus, and it was revealed to him in a vision that this was indeed the Tomb of St James the Apostle, with which the place had, through folk-memory, always retained legendary associations.

King Alfonso II covered the great discovery with a little church of stone and plaster. Many miracles followed, and the place was made the nucleus of a small fortified town with an abbot and twelve monks appointed to guard it.

It calls for some imagination to realise the enormous stimulus these miraculous happenings afforded the struggling, pitifully inadequate Christian forces in northern Spain – enough even to bring about victory in the Battle of Clavíjo, near Nájera and the modern Logroño, in 845. Santiago appeared on horseback and personally slew 6,000 (or, as some say, 60,000) Moors and, in gratitude, King Ramiro I proclaimed St James the

* *Campus Stellae* = starry field = Compostela.

patron saint of Spain.

(The battle was provoked by the refusal of the Christians to pay a tribute of 100 virgins demanded by the Emir of Cordoba, and historians only destroy the mood of the Golden Legend by insisting that the forces sent to collect an agreed tribute would hardly have been sufficiently large to supply the Saint with 6,000 – let alone 60,000 – Moors to slay.)

The news of the victory was circulated with an order from the king to all churches throughout Spain to pay the Abbey of Santiago de Compostela an annual tribute of wine and corn and, this being Spain, the tribute was punctually paid until the year 1812!

Alfonso III (the Great), who reigned from 866 till 910, declared a Holy War, and built a cathedral at Compostela, with three naves and three apses, one each for Our Lord, St Peter and St John, which immediately became the spiritual capital of Christian Spain, and his successor Ramiro II, after winning the Battle of Simancas in 939, freed much of the surrounding land from which it could expect to be menaced by later Moslem attacks.

However, disasters soon followed. First some raiding Normans captured Compostela in 968, and held it for two years and then – far worse – the fell shadow of Almanzor-el-Allah (the Spanish rendering of Abu Amir Muhammad Al-Mansur) loomed over not only Compostela, but menaced the entire achievement of the Reconquest.

He entered Compostela on August 10 of the year 997 and found it deserted. He totally destroyed the Cathedral, but could find no trace of the body of the Apostle. A Moorish source recounts, however, that Almanzor found an old man sitting on the Tomb who said, 'I am a familiar of St James, and I am saying my prayers,' to which the conquering Moslem replied, 'Pray on. No man shall molest you,' and placed a strong guard around the place to ensure his promise being kept, but when he returned the old man had vanished, though none of the guard had seen him go.

Whether St James remained undisturbed, or at least undiscovered, we do not know, but Almanzor's triumph was complete, and when he returned to Córdoba, hundreds of

Christian slaves dragged the huge bells captured from the Cathedral across the width of Spain. Once there, the bells were hung upside-down and used as oil lamps in the enormous mosque, a process reversed by the Saint-King Ferdinand after his defeat of the Emirate in 1236, when they were hauled all the way back to Compostela by Moorish prisoners.

Almanzor died blind five years after his victory, but some felt that St James had not handled matters very convincingly, and St Isidor, whose body was found by the King of Leon at the capture of Seville, was preferred by El Cid to assist him in his relief of hard pressed Coimbra – but St James remained Spain's patron saint, and the great war-cry of 'Santiago, y cierra España'* was to sound across countless bloody battle-fields until the last of the Moors had been expelled.

Here, as I have already said, we are firmly on the Pilgrim's Way, though the Way itself allows, indeed encourages detours to individual monasteries, churches or hospitals, and few among them are without their representations of the pilgrims themselves, with their gay companions the *juglares* – in French, *jongleurs* – who literally sang for their suppers, provid-ing tales of ancient days or recent rumours of the contempor-arily Great Ones according to their patrons' tastes. Often pass-ing craftsmen on the pilgrimage, sculptors and painters, would voluntarily make a contribution to a church wall or porch along the way, and it is they who have recreated the daily life of the period and place as no written words could have done.

First are the pilgrims themselves, with their unmistakable scallop shell badges, shady hats, water bottles, square bread boxes and long staves. Here, too, are the *juglares*, the gipsies and even the bandits, all marching in a Magical world of time-less movement, and you will occasionally catch sight of one of the 13 Knights of St James, authorised by Pope Alexander III in 1175 to protect the pilgrims against attacks from highwaymen. You will find that renderings of 'The Weighing of Souls' is a recurring theme – the 'goodies' looking too smug for words as they watch the 'baddies' being sent below for roasting.

Feeling that I deserved a couple of days to rest and sort out my impressions, I took the road from Sangüesa for the short

* Roughly, 'St James, and close ranks for Spain'. c.s.

run southwest to the little town of Tafalla and thence for the walking distance on to the parador of Olite. Thereby I discovered much that was new to me, and would otherwise have missed. In Spain it is rarely wise to hurry! From here you can wander through one of the least known and best encastled areas in the entire country, and never even see a package tour.

My proposed two days rest turned out to be four days of exploration – but the accidental chance was too good to miss.

First of all the fifteenth-century Castle of Olite itself would have been worth the effort. Once the royal residence of the Kings of Navarre, walled, and with many square towers, it is a place to remember, and Mine Host, warned of my peculiarities, was adamant that I must postpone my rendezvous with Charlemagne at the Pass of Roncesvalles until I had seen Puente la Reina, Tafala and most particularly, Estella once known as Estella la Bella – not to mention a brace of local monasteries or abbeys. As he backed up his arguments with copious draughts of red Rioja – unquestionably Spain's finest table wine – it is possible that I was not particularly difficult to persuade!

But I took things rather less strenuously than I had done since leaving Ordesa. The following day, being a Sunday, I strolled across to the little church, passing the twelfth-century San Pedro, with its Romanesque portal and cloister, to enter Santa Maria la Real, as I had heard of its wonderful fifteenth-century *retablo* and widely venerated image of El Cristo de la Buena Muerte. After a noble lunch, and more Rioja, my kind host himself drove me over 11 miles of bad road to the once mighty Cistercian Abbey of La Liva which, since its foundation in 1134, has contained, and still contains, a hostel (for men only) free of charge – though hardly of Hilton standards! With its pointed arches the church it believed to be the earliest example of Gothic in Spain, and the chapter house of the fifteenth century has been faultlessly restored by the Cistercian monks who still live there.

It is no distance from Olite to Tafalla – today a forgotten little town, though once, for a short while, the capital of Navarre, and known as La Flor de Navarra – the Flower of Navarre. It is somewhat overwhelmed by the great ruined fortress of Santa Lucia, but it contains a lovely old church and a street of nobly emblazoned mansions. From Tafalla my way ran west to Larraga, where it crossed the River Arga and, forking right, it was not long until I saw what I knew would be the octagonal Hermitage of Eunati, once the property of the Knights Templar, surrounded by a cloister dating from the twelfth century. Just beyond it lies the great pilgrim gathering place of Puente la Reina and the main road from Pamplona to Logroño.

I found Puente la Reina securely enfolded in its thirteenth-century walls, and paid my respects to Romanesque San Pedro and Del Crucifija – the latter also the work of the Knights Templar, and containing a very moving image of Christ.

I am always glad to see signs of the Knights Templar, who seem to me to have been given a distinctly crooked deal. Their fate was that, while there were Moors around for them to fight, they were treated as heroes, and were promised (if first they conquered them) vast lands and properties by monarchs who, without their help, were trembling in their shoes. Then, with the expulsion of the last of the Moors from France, Portugal and most of Spain, they administered their freely gifted lands with skill and energy, and so became rich.

Inevitably, with the Moorish threat removed, and abbeys, monasteries and farms prosperous, the descendants of those monarchs who a couple of centuries earlier had jumped through hoops to secure the services of this great fighting monastic order – themselves impoverished by inane wars and general mismanagement – turned against their former deliverers. Philippe le Bel of France was the chief propagandist, and accused the Knights Templar of every crime in the book, from homosexuality to Black Magic and, to save his own face, urged all other European monarchs to do the same as a preliminary to seizure of their lands and wealth, and the ultimate total disbandment of the order in the fourteenth century.

My indignation on their behalf was only decreased on this occasion by the consumption of most of a minute suckling pig – its crackling made crisp by basting, during its slow turning on the spit over an olivewood fire, in a mixture of brandy and rum – at the Inn beside the ancient pilgrim's bridge, which was erected just 16 years before our Battle of Hastings.

The, by now, unfamiliar delight of driving on a motor road made the 11-mile run to Estella seem even less than I had expected and, once there I finally and fully forgave my host of the parador at Olite for having turned me aside from my original itinerary.

Estella is so rich in beauty that it has sometimes been called 'the Toledo of the North' – though I greatly deplore the general tendency to make these kind of comparisons. (How many dreary Eastern capitals merely emphasise their dreariness by insisting that they are 'the Paris of the Balkans'?) However, like Toledo, Estella would qualify for that other depressing title of being 'a museum city' if she were stupid enough to apply for it. Fortunately it is small, so it does not overwhelm and confuse me as, quite frankly, Toledo does, unless I take it in small doses over a period of days.

I realise that I have led you into rather more churches and monasteries than is to everyone's taste but, with a half dozen magnificent exceptions, such as Santo Domingo de la Calzada, Burgos and Leon, the need to do so grows less after we reach the sea.

You approach Estella over the 'pilgrim's bridge' built by King Sanchez Ramirez, which is a good start. It seems that he created an agreement between the Kings of Aragon, Navarre, Castile and Leon that they would all do all that seemed possible to keep the Pilgrim's Way, through each of their territories, in good condition, with bridges, hospitals, hostels and churches at every key point, and the bridge at Estella was one of his personal contributions to the scheme.

Another was the Abbey of Irache, which was a university until as late as 1851. There it was the custom that when one of the community died then each of the surviving brethren would say seven masses for the repose of his soul, and the Abbey fed 30 poor pilgrims, and for 30 days a pilgrim was free to sleep in the dead man's cell and draw his rations free of charge.

In all religions you tend to find actions which, while they have no direct connection with the deity, are undertaken as Acts of Virtue. I observed while in Burma that the building of a pagoda was the same, the donor expecting to 'acquire merit', but not necessarily any kind of reward, either here or in the hereafter.

The origins of Estella are lost in antiquity, but it is believed to have been built upon the Ibero-Roman town of Gabala. Here, too, died the Bishop of Patras in 1270 and, since he was under oath of silence for the duration of the pilgrimage, he was buried in the common ground assigned for those who died along the way to Santiago. However, the very same night, clustering lights appeared over his grave and, after due deliberation, his body was exhumed. It was then found that he was carrying a shoulder-blade of St Andrew, its authenticity duly attested by the Pope, and this was placed in a golden reliquary by King Carlos II – rather unkindly referred to in local history as 'the Bad'!

The mediaeval Kings of Navarre encouraged the Jews to settle in Estella – there is still a large ghetto—and it enjoyed great prosperity until Ferdinand and Isabella introduced the Inquisition late in the fifteenth century. It escaped the disasters of the Carlist Wars from 1833–9 and from 1872–6 by the simple process of becoming the Carlist headquarters.

Estella is so rich in antiquity that I will only mention the few things that remain most strongly in my own memory. There is the rounded arch of thirteenth-century San Miguel, with its original wrought ironwork doors and richly carved tympanum; twelfth-century San Pedro de la Rua with a charming Romanesque cloister and, in its Treasury, an ancient bronze crozier with Limoges enamels of the same period as the church itself. San Juan Bautisto has some exquisite baroque retablos, and the lovely and loving Virgin of Rocamadour in the Capuchin Convent on a height just outside the city walls. Wander where you will, through the twelfth-century Palace of the Dukes of Granada and the Renaissance Palace of the Counts of San Cristobal without fear that you will meet anything unsightly, and I will lay long odds against your seeing a single tourist, packaged or in the raw, who will stop between Pamplona and Longroño – except, perhaps, to obey a sudden call of nature!

You will probably choose to run northwest for a comfortable night in Pamplona and thence, north or northwest to the

sea either at the frontier or, if you are following me into Spain,
inevitably, San Sebastian. It so happened that I had to return to
my parador at Olite for the night and thence, by devious
routes, make my way through Aoiz and Burguete to Roncesvalles before turning back, later and tireder than you, to Pamplona.

To be honest, Roncesvalles came as something of a disappointment to me, but it was, as it were, on my conscience, as
I had been near to it so often and yet, for some reason or other,
always failed to visit it.

The village of Roncesvalles – a bare two miles below an out-
thrust of the French frontier line – has not a great deal to
show, and most of that was obscured on this occasion by what
is politely called a Scotch mist – cheerless, damp and draining
away all colour from the scene.

However, it was the route chosen by most invading or retreating armies throughout the centuries. The high Pyrenees
now lie to the southeast, and Roncesvalles, only some 3,600
feet above sea level, must have seemed preferable to the more
obvious, but very narrow, and presumably well-defended
coastal strip but, even to an amateur, the opportunity for am-
bush which it provided should have been obvious.

The Romans, at least to begin with, came along the Mediterranean, and the Moors, of course, across the Straits to Tariq's
Rock, now called Gibraltar, but nearly all the rest, conquerors
and conquered, chose this route.

First the Goths, Visigoths and Vandals came surging into the
vacuum caused by the collapse of Roman rule – large, beefy,
malodorous types, themselves fleeing from pressures by the
Huns – soon Christianised by those they had conquered and,
hamstrung by the evils of an elected, as distinct from an
hereditary monarchy, soon themselves to fall victim to the
Moors.

Charlemagne came this way unopposed, indeed invited, by
the people of Zaragoza, and it was only his rearguard, on their
way home, that was wiped out by rocks rolled down upon
them, followed by a murderous attack from an enemy hidden
above them – supposedly Basques – though there is evidence to

suggest that the Navarrese played some part in it in anger at the terrible deprivations caused by the Franks.

The accuracy of the famous epic poem telling us of the slaying of Roland the Fair and all his men is, like that of all epic poems, somewhat suspect, firstly because it was not written until some 400 years after the event and secondly because, even then, it was written for French audiences, with an understandable emphasis upon the noble behaviour of Roland and the twelve peers of France, rather than upon their criminal negligence in having failed to scout the surrounding heights before entering the narrowest part of the defile!

In any case the defeat seems to have shaken the great Charlemagne – that giant of a man with the high, weak voice – and when Louis (the Debonair) came the same way 32 years later, in 810, he took the trouble first to catch the wives and children of the local tribesmen, and force them to accompany him until the Pass widened sufficiently to allow his men to deploy.

Our Black Prince led his troops through here in 1367 to assist Pedro the Cruel to regain his throne from Enrique de Trastamara in the Battle of Nájera and, in 1813, Napoleon's Marshal Soult employed this route in an unsuccessful attempt at a surprise attack upon Wellington to relieve Pamplona.

Today there is little to see but a damp-stained thirteenth-century Augustinian abbey containing the Tombs of King Sancho (the Strong) of Navarre and his Queen Clemencia, together with two links of the great chain he broke at the Battle of Las Navas de Toloso, and various magnificent mediaeval reliquaries. In the Treasury is a gold embroidered cope presented by the Saint-Queen Elizabeth of Portugal who, born Spanish, made the full pilgrimage to Santiago de Compostela on foot after the death of her husband, King Diniz, in the fourteenth century. Opposite the Abbey is the twelfth-century Capilla del Espirito Santo and, near by, the ancient parish church of Santiago which, rather surprisingly, is no longer in use.

The most attractive thing about the place, speaking only from hearsay, is the 'romaria' every year on the Wednesday before Whitsun of penitents who climb barefoot to the head of this gloomy pass, bearing heavy wooden crosses upon their shoulders.

As I drove cautiously down the corkscrew road towards Pamplona I wondered vaguely why, if you speak of the Basque Country to an Englishman, he always assumes that you are talking about the tiny corner of France in which the Basques are found, and not of the very considerable area, covered by the provinces of Guipúzcoa, Vizcaya (from which comes the name of the Biscay of the Bay), Álava and northern Navarre, with their natural capital of Bilbao, all on the Spanish side of the frontier. Similarly, if you say that you are going to visit the Pyrenees – or make a walking tour in the foothills – they suggest Cauterets, or perhaps Bagnères de Bigorre as providing a good base, apparently not aware that at least three-quarters of the Pyrenees are Spanish, and not French possessed.

The truth of this latter point I remember having demonstrated to me when, long ago, I reached the top of the Cirque de Gavarnie, just on the border and, looking north, could see – admittedly in the far distance and on a very clear day – green fields under cultivation and then, turning to look south, saw only range upon range of mountains to the farthest horizon.

The lights and warmth of Pamplona are welcome now, even as they must have been to the many British soldiers smuggled over the border by the faithful Basques in 1940 and, later, when the Germans moved into the hitherto 'Unoccupied Zone' of southern France.

There has always been a natural affinity between the British and the Basques, just as there has always been an almost total non-comprehension between the British and the Spanish. One obvious reason is that we tend to like our foreigners – since, unfortunately, foreigners are inevitable – to be simple and, if possible, devoted to playing games, or indulging in sports, where the rules are unnecessarily complicated, and who are preferably, hearty eaters and drinkers. It makes us feel gratifyingly superior, whereas the intensely reserved, almost archaic formality and courtesy of the Spanish peasant often seems to most of my compatriots to be a cloak for something like contempt. In fact it is due to other and very different reasons – such as, for example, the agonising fear that you are going to try to patronise him – but all this becomes more obvious as we penetrate more profoundly into what the Phoenicians so perceptively called 'The Hidden Land'.

But our objective now is Pamplona and, if you are young, choose the famous Fiesta de San Fermin, when the bulls are coursed through the streets to the bullring for the *entrar en los chiqueros** leading up to the *encierro*, or shutting up of the bulls in their separate stalls, ready to be released into the ring at the great moment.

The Fiesta de San Fermin is one long orgy of wild dancing, deafening fireworks, gargantuan drinking and hurried love-making, all of which was brilliantly described by Hemingway, and a list of less brilliant authors, to the inordinate length of which I will make no attempt to add. All that it is necessary for me to note here is that between July 5 and 16 you will get no sleep in Pamplona, but it is a tremendous experience just once, while you are young but, emphatically, only for the under-35s. The mad flight before the horns of the angry black bulls carries a real and contagious excitement which the professional performers in the ring can rarely induce, and it attracts the hearty basques from all their provinces. It is rare that anyone gets killed, though there are often a dozen or so more or less seriously hurt. It is, apparently, an acceptable price to pay as homage to their dutifully impressed girlfriends watching from the balconies.

Pamplona was built around 68 B.C. by the sons of Pompey, and named Pompeiopolis and followed the familiar path of Roman, Gothic and Moslem occupation, but the tough Navarrese, striking back from their mountain fastnesses, liberated the city after only 12 years. However, Moorish pressure became so intolerable that they joined with the Christians of Zaragoza to implore help from the great Emperor Charlemagne but, as we already know, the devastation he caused during his attempts to capture the Aragonese capital convinced them that the remedy was worse than the disease – hence Roncesvalles!

Even so Navarre was a Kingdom in 905, when Pamplona became the capital of Sancho I, and remained so – apart from

* *entrar en los chiqueros*: preview of the fighting bulls for VIPs and managers of the *toreros* to take part.

9   *The quiet river Iregua (Logroño) waters the vines which produce the best red wines of Spain*

10 *Santillana del Mar (Santander), where the high Castilian
plateau has run down to the sea*

short periods of French occupation – until the ageing Ferdinand, widower of Isabella of Castile, drove Queen Catalina out in 1512, and fierce attempts to regain possession by her husband, Jean d'Albret, with French assistance, finally failed in 1521.

Incidentally, it was in the fighting for Pamplona that a Basque nobleman named Iñigo Lopez de Recalde was gravely wounded and, when slowly recovering, received the inspiration that was to turn him into St Ignatius de Loyola, founder of the counter-reformationist Order of Jesus – the Jesuits – at whose house we will call briefly later.

Basically Pamplona is not a town which gives the casual visitor any great sense of antiquity, and you can do your serious sightseeing in a few hours. The Throne Room contains portraits of the Kings, or ruling Queens of Navarre – though the early ones obviously present only apocryphal likenesses, and some of them had also been Kings of Aragon – and the Cathedral, though dating back to 1023, only acquired its present form in 1783, and is a cold place both physically and spiritually.

However, the Tomb of Carlos III, who died in 1425, and his Queen Leonora of Castile, carved by Lomme of Tournai, is an imposing example of the Burgundian style with a procession of 'mourners' round the pedestal. The Grille to the Capilla Mayor (Main Chapel) completed in 1517, seems remarkable until you can compare it with others in Spain, and the Virgin de los Reyes on the High Altar, before which the Kings of Navarre kept vigil throughout the night before their coronation, is of immense age.

However you should take a look at the Sala Preciosa ('Beautiful Room') which opens off the fourteenth-century cloisters of the Cathedral, and was the meeting place of the Cortes, or Parliament, of Navarre. Additionally, in the little Capilla de la Santa Cruz, it is interesting to know that the Grille was forged entirely from the pavilion tent-chains of the Moorish Emir captured at the Battle of Las Navas de Tolosa in 1212. Beyond is the delightful Refectory of the Canons, now sacred to St Francis Xavier, leading into the old kitchens, with the typical vast open hearth and chimney which, to a generation resigned to cooking on a gas ring, has always suggested, perhaps correctly, that the clergy of the Middle Ages devoted an excessive amount of their time and wealth to eating and drinking.

But Spain is a land of superb cathedrals and churches, and that of Pamplona is emphatically nowhere near to being among the best. In all Spain the only 'compulsory' ones are those of Toledo, Seville, Burgos, Leon and Santiago de Compostela, though there are more, many more, which are of very real interest or beauty. The 'Cathedral' of Cordoba, for example, is the most beautiful mosque west of Istanbul!

Pamplona is a pleasant enough place, cool at nights due to its 1,500 feet, but never one that has lured me into a long stay, and on this journey I was soon on my way towards San Sebastian, 67 miles to the sea which I had not seen since leaving Barcelona.

4. The Hearty Basques

San Sebastian, twelve miles from the once-famous International Bridge over the River Bidasoa into France, is the Spanish attempt to compete with Biarritz, an hour's drive away, though the creation of the Empress Eugénie in the eighteen sixties has always had the edge on that of the Spanish Queen Regent Maria Cristina in the eighteen nineties, largely because, in France, a gambling casino may be legal whereas, except intermittently, it is not in Spain.

However it has two beautifully sheltered sandy bathing beaches (which Biarritz has not) and, from July 18th until October 1st it is, quite officially, the capital of Spain – Madrid between those dates being like a cement oven – but, despite all this and film festivals too, there is still something faintly pre-World War One about San Sebastian. One's grandparents would, I feel, have described it – in the days before 'bathing resorts' had been invented – as 'a charming watering place'!

Through its midst winds the River Urumea, dividing the area of beach hotels, smart boutiques and official buildings from the 'Old Town' – though, by Spanish standards it is not very old, even if there are Son et Lumière performances before the sixteenth-century Convent of San Telmo, during the *Semana Grande** in August. On the last occasion when I was in San Sebastian for the Semana Grande I remember a rather surprising combination of bullfights, regattas and Artur Rubinstein piano recitals!

At least here, in San Sebastian, you can find the Basque cuisine at its best – and at its best it can be very good indeed by

* *Semana Grande*, literally 'Big Week', i.e. the high spot of the Season.

any standards. The subject is taken very seriously. There are dozens of clubs – for men only – where a member may go in order himself to cook his favourite dishes in his favourite way. Being a mountain people, confronting a cold winter climate, the end product is pretty filling by British, or even by French standards, and pays no attention whatsoever to the preservation of your vital statistics.

Naturally they take advantage of the local fish, both shell and ordinary, and the *homard* here advantageously replaces the slightly rubbery *langouste* of the Mediterranean. Fresh anchovies,* baked and dressed spider crab au gratin, grilled sea-bream, *merluza en salsa verde*, and tiny, baby squid (*pulpitos*) – all abound to tempt your palate and, probably, put up your blood pressure.

The Basques – like the Portuguese, but unlike the Spaniards – make use of *bacalau* which, unattractive though it may sound, is salted cod caught off the stormy coasts of Newfoundland. On sale it appears about as appetising as a cricket bat, and is of a similar texture, but with it as a foundation many delicious dishes can be concocted. Most meats seem to be cooked in wine and, almost always, are not entirely innocent of garlic which, fortunately for me (though, perhaps, less so for my friends) I happen to like.

The really great speciality of the district, which I personally consider one of the world's most exquisite dishes, is *angulas a la bilbaina*, eel spawn, or elvas – the length of your little finger, but no thicker than a matchstick – which are caught only at the point where a river becomes tidal. Cooked in a little of the finest olive oil, together with an unbroken clove of garlic and a sliver of flaming hot red pepper, all served with the oil still boiling in the small earthenware dish in which they have been prepared, and eaten with wooden forks – the touch of metal destroys the flavour – they really are a gastronomic delight!

The rivers of the Basque country also provide plenty of trout, salmon and salmon-trout, but such conventional delicacies are far outshone by the fresh-water crayfish, which abound all the way to Burgos.

Never more than six inches long, and plain boiled in pep-

* *Bocartes a la Papillote* is how they will feature on the menu.

pered water containing various herbs, it looks exactly like its salt-water brother, but with a disproportionately large head, and the flavour is out of this world. Only here and in Rumania have I ever been able to eat as many of these delicate fresh-water shellfish as I wished. One is almost prompted to wonder whether they were an added, if minor, inducement, prompting the faithful to undertake the long and dangerous pilgrimage to Compostela.

The Basques also know about cheeses – strong, smelly and liable to snap back at you – none of the bland imitation Dutch, or unfermented goat stuff which the Spaniards favour!

It is remarkable that no one should be able to trace the origins of a race so distinctive as the Basques, particularly as their language is completely unlike any other, being notable only for the fact that it obeys no known laws of grammar and is almost completely unpronounceable anyway. You must not be offended if you hear such words as '*Zumalacarrequi*'. '*Irureto-goyena*' and '*Utiaquereca*', nor, even, if you are invited to dance the *aurresku* or – seemingly worse – the *purrusalda*. The locals take such tongue-twisters in their stride, while simultaneously eating scalding fresh fried sardines in their fingers, together with the heads and bones – far larger heads and bones, be it noted, than those of sardines raised genteelly for the tin.

A likely suggestion is that they are the descendants of the original Ibero-Celtic stock, which somehow survived each successive wave of invasion by retiring into the mountain fastnesses of the Pyrenees. Their reputation for inaccessibility, knowledge of every goat-track of a route, absence of loot-worthy possessions, impossible language and, if cornered, extreme ferocity, made them unattractive material for attempted genocide.

Today they are generally taller than the Spaniards and, much more often than not, heavily, but very strongly built; barrel-chested, bullet-headed, and with the thick, slightly bow-legs often to be found among mountain peoples. Naturally, like everyone these days, they have an urge towards separatism, which partly accounts for this devoutly Catholic minority cheerfully making common cause with the church-burning Catalans in 1936. Quite simply, both are against rule from

Madrid, regardless of whether Madrid was ruled by a king, a republic or by Franco.

Their ideas of recreation are as distinctive as their language. Axe races between hugely muscled lumberjacks, to see who can split up a three yard thick tree-trunk in the shortest time; stone piercing; cider and beer drinking and beef-eating competitions, are all tremendously popular sports. However, from all these slightly undergraduate examples of their general enthusiasm for all that is 'hearty' has emerged one extremely good game, commonly known as *pelota*.

The word simply means 'ball', though in their own language they call it *jai-alai*. The game, while catering for the national need to be both exhausting and fraught with complex rules, is also highly skilled and a most exciting spectacle – probably the fastest and most exhausting ball game in the world. This has, quite understandably, become so popular that *frontones*, or closed courts, have sprung up all over the country, and spread to Cuba, Mexico and most of South America, though the best players are still, almost always, Basques.

A game is always difficult to describe to anyone who has not seen it played, but I will try. The very long but narrow court is made of reinforced concrete on three out of its four sides, the fourth being out-of-bounds and covered with strong wire netting, and so open to the watching and seated public.

The players, usually two pairs (with a blue or red sash to distinguish one pair from the other) wear a kind of glove attached to their right wrists, and the entire game is played backhand along the further wall – except for an accident in placement – though the left hand may be used to impart still greater power and speed to the shot hurled from the basket on the other towards the distant back wall of the court (above a certain marked line as in squash-rackets). As the entire game is played, as I have already said, on the hardest possible surface the speed at which the ball – hard, and slightly smaller than a cricket ball – travels is quite incredible.

There is passionate betting on the game, with the odds varying according to the fortunes of play, the 'bookies', in white jackets, standing with their backs to the game (but with a beady eye on the score-board) accepting bets at the rates they are currently yelling. At a signal from you they will instantly toss you a soft rubber ball with a hole in it. Into this you insert the amount you wish to bet saying whether it is 'red' or 'blue' that you favour, and return it to him – probably with considerably less accuracy than he originally flipped it to you – when he pockets your money, and makes a note of receipt both in his book and another for you, delivered by the same method, to enable you to collect if you happen to win.

If anyone could think of a more complex method either of playing the game or of betting on its outcome, then I am sure that the Basques would welcome the suggestion with enthusiasm. But, whatever the complications, it is tremendous fun to watch.

On an earlier visit to this part of Spain, made later in the year, I was persuaded into taking part in the Basque idea of a pigeon shoot. Of late I have felt less and less pleasure in killing things (except for the pot, or an occasional creditor) but, knowing the Basques, I was certain that they would have worked out a method so complicated as to enable a large number of pigeons to survive. I was right.

The scene of operations was right on the frontier, and required special permits. To begin with I had to be ready at 6 a.m., and so missed my breakfast, and was then driven inland beside the River Bidasoa along a winding, muddy side-road to within a couple of hundred yards of the neck of the 1,500-foot Pass of Echalar, where there was a simple restaurant and a few mountain huts connected with the sport. Climbing another hundred yards on foot we gazed down on the French village of Sare and, as the light strengthened, away to the sea at Biarritz.

Between mid-October and mid-November every year hundreds of thousands of pigeons leave their summer breeding-grounds, mostly around the Baltic, and begin their great migration to northern Africa. Their direct line takes them across France to this northeast corner of Spain. They avoid traversing long distances over the sea – the narrow Baltic and the Straits of Gibraltar do not take them out of sight of land – but they now find themselves confronted by the huge mountain wall of the Pyrenees, through which the Pass of Echalar offers the lowest passage. Although tens of thousands cross by other routes, the majority make for the narrow break where I was standing, which was rendered even narrower by the planting of tall trees on either side of a grassy gap, across which were stretched nets 80 feet high, which drop to the ground as soon as a flock or covey strikes it, imprisoning the pigeons in its ample, falling folds.

Ingenious though this is, the birds would rarely fly into the nets if they were not cunningly encouraged to do so. Far down the narrowing valley ending at the pass men were stationed in masked coverts and, as a flight of two or three dozen birds drew level, they blew bugles, beat drums, and generally made as much din as possible to scare them in the desired direction. If the birds were flying too high to be caught by the nets, then men flung flat white wooden disks, looking like badly made ping-pong bats, curving through the air above them. Mistaking these for diving hawks, the pigeons swerved away and downwards, while continuing upon their same line of flight.

There are obviously various other and far easier methods of obtaining pigeons, if pigeons were really the primary object of the operation. However, being Basques, they preferred to invent this uniquely complicated method, involving dozens of people, including myself, swarming up and down muddy mountains at an hour when we all ought to have been ordering breakfast in bed.

However, there is a kind of breathless excitement in waiting for the next flock to appear against a cold white, early-morning sky, and it is unquestionably sporting, in that quite half the birds escape. Anyway I am extremely fond of a lunch of pigeon stewed in a savoury sauce, and I was glad personally to reduce the morning's bag of 368 birds by three.

On this present visit I had a sentimental journey to make to the mouth of the River Bidasoa, above the International Bridge, and this was made the easier by the Parador of Fuentarrabia, which did not exist in the days which I had come here to recall. It stands high, overlooking the river and the French coast – Hendaye, St Jean de Luz and, on clear days, even Bayonne to the east, but north of it is an immensely long promontory, known as Cape Higuer, to the west of which I once spent a chilly and uncomfortable 20 hours, secretly housed in a leaky cow-shed.

When Franco captured Barcelona late in January 1939 all foreign newspapermen (with the example of Koestler in mind) fled across the French frontier, with the exception of myself and the Reuter's man, Bill Williams, who had a Catalan wife. Naturally, it was not long before I was summoned by the new Press Chief – a pleasant enough man called Llambari, selected for the job as he had been a noted landscape painter. My newspaper had been doing its best for me, cabling the new authorities to say how highly they regarded me but, unfortunately, adding that I had 'always reported the war objectively'. Although their motives were above reproach, they could hardly have employed a more damaging phrase!

A Spaniard, if he does not kill him first, can enjoy an emotional reconciliation with his worst enemy, but 'objectivity' he universally regards as one of the Seven Deadly Sins'!

However, once delivered, under guard, in Burgos, I found that my fate was in the hands of the Marqués Merry del Val, who had been educated in England at Stonyhurst, and whose father had once been Ambassador to the Court of St James, and so was a man who could understand such Anglo-Saxon peculiarities as objectivity, and even that a professional newspaperman did not have to be a Communist to have reported the war from the 'Red' side. Incidentally, he paid me one of the highest compliments I have ever received by saying that, out of the hundred or so foreign correspondents on the two sides during the war, only three were not classified as either 'red' or 'white', and that I was one of these three! My 'sentence' therefore consisted of three days' holiday in San Sebastian 'on the house'; the right to return to Barcelona to collect my possessions, but a total prohibition upon working in Spain until the war was ended – which it obviously would be in a matter of weeks.

In fact, after my three days in San Sebastian and return to Barcelona, I went briefly to London, and then took a rather more extended holiday at Sare –a charming little French town close to the frontier.

Seven months later I was in desperate flight from Warsaw to neutral Rumania but, odd though it may seem to us today, the

British newspaper public in May and June 1939 was deeply anxious to know whether or not Franco's victory being complete, the German technicians and, to a lesser extent, Italian troops were, or were not leaving Spain.

Since it was too early for me to work again officially in Spain I decided that I would engage some reliable Basques to smuggle me in – and out – for a period long enough for me to be able to answer this question.

By methods which are probably of no great interest to any reader of this book, I will merely say that, after a while, I found myself in a small wine tavern in Hendaye for inspection by the 'Chief'. The floor was of beaten earth, while around the smoke-stained walls were a dozen vast wooden casks, cobwebbed and black with age. The single table was stained with wine; the conversation quiet, almost whispered, and in Basque.

The 'Chief' (who many escaping British airmen were to meet after Dunkirk) was surprisingly young, and our conversation brief and satisfactory. For a payment of what was then the equivalent of £7 he promised to get me to San Sebastian, and gave me a code to enable me to contact their man there when I was ready to leave on my return journey.

Forty-eight hours later I left the Café Basque, where I had had a magnificent dinner in anticipation that, apart from scraps, it might be my last good meal for some days, and strolled unobtrusively towards the unfashionable quarter that lies near the old port. It was a moonless night, but I had no difficulty in finding the corner where I had been told to be at eleven o'clock. A figure detached itself from a doorway opposite and, without a word, guided me by the elbow through a garden gate to the back entrance of a house that bore a large 'For Sale' notice. In the basement four figures were handling several large, square bales which, later I learned, contained silk and tobacco. They took no notice of me until they left, when one of them said, 'directly you hear three whistles walk slowly across the road towards the sea, and someone will guide you to the boat'.

A moment later I had heard the signal, crossed the road, and was stumbling across a short section of lumpy grass until I saw the boat below me, moored against a partly ruined stone wall. I found a place aft upon one of the bales, and immediately the boat put off. The oars were muffled, and we slid through the ink-black water across the harbour and towards the open sea in total silence, two men rowing while a third kept a lookout in the bows.

Soon the strong rise and fall of the Atlantic showed that we were clear of France, but were rowing towards what appeared to me to be an all-seeing blaze of light on the end of this great headland of Cape Higuer. That headland was in Spain. Slowly we were creeping round this locked frontier which might be hiding the answer to so many things I wished to know.

It was three o'clock before we passed round and out of sight of that infernally brilliant lighthouse, and the boat was now headed towards the white markings of broken water where it surged around the foot of black cliffs. The look-out man was tensely alert for some signal from that wild-looking coast. It came – a single flash from a dark lantern above us – and the men at the oars again drove the boat towards the faint white of the breaking surf.

A few moments later the keel scraped lightly on stones, and a strong, hard hand came out of the dark, pulled me ashore, and up a stiff grass track that left me gasping for breath, but with my feet once again on Spanish soil despite all the vigilant *Guardias* that lined the frontier.

After the bales of contraband had been cached in some thick bushes my invisible companion returned, and handed me a goatskin of harsh red wine. I raised it and squirted a jet on to the back of my throat in the approved style.

My companions from Hendaye had all gone about their secret business, and for me the next two hours had the quality of a dream. Mile after mile of rough tussocky grass was made doubly difficult since the inequalities of the surface were invisible. How my guide managed it, with a heavy bale on his back, I cannot imagine – except, of course, that he was a Basque. Once in a while his hand would stop me and force me down into a squatting position for a moment of complete silence. Then there would come a low whistle out of the dark, often from a considerable distance, and we would set off again. The route we were following must have been picketed by at least a dozen men on the alert for Guardias, but I never saw one of them.

Near dawn I was feeling pretty weary. At last we came to a low, partly ruined cowshed, the floor covered by earth and dung, but empty.

'Sleep,' said my guide, whom I had never seen. 'Food will be brought you during the day, and tomorrow night you will be on your way to San Sebastian.' With a murmured '*buenas noches*' he was gone, and I was left in complete blackness but, exhausted by my long climb, I soon dozed off.

I awoke to a heavy drizzling rain. The roof of the cow-shed was leaking in several places, and outside the grey hilltop was visible for a bare hundred yards. In those days I smoked, and I sat up in the thin light, lit a pipe, and wondered why I had this deplorable tendency for getting myself into the most absurd positions. I swore, as often I had sworn before – and was later to swear in Poland, Jakarta, Burma and Angola in the years to follow – that if I ever got out of this I would change my way of life, and do something nice, conventional and safe.

A shepherd brought me some hard-boiled eggs and cider in mid-morning, and I did my best to arouse interest in a novel in which the characters seemed to have nothing better to do than to torture themselves and each other by quite unnecessarily refraining from the simple, indeed admirable, act of copulation. It took them 350 pages to get safely to bed, and I wondered what the hero would have done if he had found himself on the top of a Spanish mountain, surrounded by armed Guardias who would get promoted if they found him sitting in a damp cowshed with no reasonable explanation of how he had got there.

However, it all ended happily and, after four days in San Sebastian, I had all the facts and figures for which I had come in search. The Germans and the Italians *were* pulling out fast, and a week after leaving Hendaye, I was once more being rowed round this great headland, with its uncomfortably brilliant light still appearing to point directly at me.

On this present journey it took me some time to find my cowshed, but I found it at last, shiny and repaired, and shriven of any guilt for having once inadequately sheltered an inquisitive foreign correspondent.

This rather dangerous hide-and-seek frontier game seems to be endemic among the Basques, and sometimes produces humorous incidents which in retrospect delight both 'cops and robbers', and I was the non-participating observer of one of these when, for a while in the fifties, my wife and I had a delightful and incredibly inexpensive furnished cottage in Zarauz, some 15 miles west of San Sebastian, when the winter was enlivened by the activities of the '*fantasma negra*'.

Now, as anyone knows, a black ghost is far worse than the common-or-garden white or grey variety, and requires a whole collection of bells, books and candles before it can be successfully exorcised.

To begin with, it was only a few old women who staggered in babbling complaints to the Guardia Civil Headquarters (and some unkind souls even suggested that it was an act put on just in order to obtain a large free brandy). But when one of the town's two doctors – a man of scientific training – was brought in, pale and trembling, the authorities decided that they must act. The doctor had been returning late from an emergency case in Cestora when one of the front tyres of his car went flat near a small railway bridge. Getting out to inspect, he was aware of a voice behind him that said,

'Tonight you have saved a life. Meet me here at the same hour tomorrow, or you will pay me back with your own.'

Wheeling round, the good doctor perceived a tall black figure motionless beside him. The next thing he knew was that he was driving as fast as he could on his flat tyre, regardless of the wheel rim and the outer cover. Of course he did not believe in ghosts, black or otherwise, but really it was difficult to accept the idea that anyone would play such a profitless practical joke!

The Captain of the Civil Guard did some hard thinking and announced, 'Well, whatever it was that you saw, it gave itself away when it told you to meet it tomorrow night. You will keep the appointment – and so will I and my entire company of six men, and we will put an end to all this "fantasma negra" business once and for all.'

Well before the appointed hour the Captain had posted his

men in strategic but concealed places with Napoleonic pre-
cision, while he and his sergeant took cover under the bridge.
Above their heads the doctor – a shivering morsel of live bait –
waited, apparently alone, for his unpleasant visitor.

The appointed hour came, and passed. For an hour longer
the waiting men stood in the cold wind and swore under their
breath. The party was then called off and returned to the village, feeling somewhat unkindly towards the doctor and his
old woman's tales. But the Captain was not satisfied, and the
following night he and the sergeant came back alone, and stationed themselves as before. It was a moonless night, and it
was some time before the sergeant's eye caught sight of something darker than the darkness among the trees. He rushed
forward, with rifle at the ready, calling upon the figure to surrender. Nothing happened, the black shape seeming only to
flap derisively in answer. Scenting promotion or martyrdom,
the sergeant hurled himself forward and bore the figure to the
ground.

By this time the Captain had caught up, and together they
examined the victim. It consisted of a skin-tight black cos-
tume, made to cover the head, in which there were slits for the
eyes, and cloak-like 'wings' attached to the shoulders. In the
single pocket they found a packet of Chesterfield cigarettes and
a hand-printed note. By the light of his torch the Captain read
as follows:

'Thanks, Captain, for your co-operation. We landed 5,000
cartons of these last night in the bay just below your quarters
while you were out catching cold – but not the Fantasma
Negra.'

However, despite so many personal memories, I did not
pause in Zarauz and its neighbour Zumaya, and turned away
from the sea on to a country road for the half-hour run to the
Monastery of Saint Ignacio de Loyola, the walls of which en-
close a part of the ancestral home, where the founder of the
Jesuit Order was born in 1491. He was born Iñigo Lopez de
Recalde, and was, as has earlier been mentioned, severely
wounded by the French while defending Pamplona in 1521 at
the age of 30. He lived to be 65, but it was during the months
of enforced idleness while recovering from this wound in a

room that you may visit on the second floor, now used as a chapel, that he conceived the whole idea of the Counter-Reformation – a kind of religious C.I.A. – though actuated by higher motives, and considerably more efficient in most of its achievements than its modern counterpart.

St Ignacio Loyala was a member of an aristocratic Basque family, whose brother's blood still runs in the veins of the present Duchess of Luna, and because he lived in the sixteenth century, far more is known of him than, for example, our Huesca friends Saints Justus and Pastor. An old soldier with a bad limp, he seems to have been both a brilliant intellectual and publicist, as well as a saint of exceptional power and personality.

In visiting his house, which is still kept more or less as though it were a private residence, I was appalled by the number of rather depressing, but presumably holy relics, which seemed to fill each room with a necrophilic gloom. I realise that these are accepted objects inspiring devotion (though emphatically not, as so many of my Protestant friends seem to believe, of idolatrous worship), but there must be enough fragments of the 'True' Cross around to have built a sizeable ship, and enough nails, supposedly employed in the Crucifixion, to have held it together. I have no wish to be irreverent, and I fully understand that an object which promotes Faith is not only desirable, but may even acquire some spiritual authenticity of its own from its association with intense belief.* However, the mania for 'holy relics' is of far later, and less credible antecedents than anything suggested in the New Testament.

What one is almost tempted to call the 'racket' in holy relics was really begun by St Helena, mother of Constantine the Great – he, who in the fourth century, moved the centre of the newly Christianised Roman Empire from Rome to Byzantium, Constantinople or Istanbul – who is credited with the discovery of the True Cross.

The story of the Crusades is full of dubious discoveries of 'Holy Lances' and 'Crowns of Thorns', 'Seamless Robes' and

* Blake explains this succinctly – 'A sincere belief that anything is so makes it so'. c.s.

'Holy Shrouds'. Soon it became something like 'keeping up with the Jones's', and every major town and church throughout Christendom simply had to have a bone or two, supposedly belonging to some holy personage, until the mania reached its peak of folly when Philip II's completely mad son was obliged to have the century-old body of a monk as his bedfellow in the hope of producing a cure!

At one time the supply of promising bones became so great as to become something of a drug on the market, and a few dozen new local saints had to be invented in order to keep the business going. The Christian Church – except for one or two corrupt Popes – was always very slow, almost reluctant, to accept all these holy bits and pieces as genuine except, as I have noted above, as objects deserving of respect since they had promoted Faith. Similarly the Vatican-appointed 'Devil's Advocate' had, and still has, the task of collecting all possible evidence *against* the claims for canonisation of new applicants for Beatitude, or outright Sainthood, and there is no doubt that St Helena never dreamed that she had created a nefarious trade, which continued for many highly profitable centuries. Naturally, some relics are perfectly genuine, but unbiased enquiry suggests that they are in the minority.

I myself, on being shown the skull of St John the Baptist in one church in France, protested that I had seen just such another attributed to St John elsewhere, and was assured that the other one was probably his when only a young man!

It was almost a relief to get away into a slightly less unhealthy form of spirituality, and I headed southwest towards Vitoria. This was still Basque country, as the place names Iparraguirre and Ormaiztegui clearly reminded me and what is, perhaps, even more dear to my heart, it is excellent stork country.

I have always had a soft spot for storks, and have noted many times that they rarely choose any but the most attractive of districts in which to nest. I have watched them, grave and immensely dignified of mien, in Spain and Turkey and, to a lesser degree in the area which used to comprise the Austro-Hungarian Empire. I share with them a considerable liking for mankind – but only for mankind when it is not oppres-

11   *Fishwives are the same in Billingsgate or Bilbao*

sively close. They seem to be respectfully treated wherever they decide to settle, and their rickety-looking, untidy nests are rarely disturbed intentionally. This was, partly, of course, due to the legend that where they are found, the family will be blessed with children. Whether or not the popularity of The Pill, plus the behaviour of the average modern child, does not threaten a change in this age-old desire to be blessed in this particular way (with a logical fall in the popularity of storks) it is hard to foresee.

Storks reveal wisdom, immense courage and, occasionally, even humour. When last I was in Istanbul I revisited the much-venerated Tomb of Mahomet's Standard Bearer in the touristically unexplored upper reaches of the Golden Horn, where there were, in addition to the Faithful, a great concourse of pigeons (the Moslem 'Little Messengers of God'), storks and cats – cats, they say, have souls, unlike dogs and women – when I observed a diminutive young stork about to begin eating a delicious piece of something revolting, when the tit-bit was suddenly whisked off by a large tom-cat. Junior was obviously downcast, but Papa had observed the incident and, with immense dignity, strolled over to a position directly behind the cat, drew back his long beak and brought its point down sharply between the ears of the offending feline – a kind of karate blow – which caused it to flee in total panic, fizzing like a leaky siphon of soda-water. Papa then inspected the disputed morsel, and indicated to an admiring Junior that he should now resume his interrupted lunch.

But I have also seen, here in Spain, that long beak thrust right through the body of an attacking eagle in what could only have been conscious suicide in defence of two wobbly-headed baby storks on the nest, which had been the objective of the eagle's attack.

And, when in Istanbul, lying on my back sunbathing beside the Bosphorus in sweltering October weather, I detected a brown, slowly swirling stain upon the cloudless sky – far higher than any smoke could possibly have risen in that form – which, after half an hour, streamed away southwest across the Sea of Marmora towards Brusa and thence, no doubt, to still warmer places like Antalya, I had no hesitation, on returning

12   *More companionable than any washing machine*

home that evening, in putting away my bathing trunks for the year. Three days later puffs of icy fog blew up the Bosphorus from the Black Sea and, in the night – 'From Russia, With Love' – there was a light fall of snow!

You will find storks a-plenty here in the Basque country, perching on crumbling fourteenth-century churches to watch a game of 'pelota' in its original form (namely against any un-windowed wall of the building, the priest, cassock belted up around his knees, batting away at the fleet, hard ball) occasionally voicelessly clapping their long beaks in unaffected applause or derision!

Anyway, I realise that not everyone shares my enthusiasm for storks; the point I was making is that you only find them in pleasant places, and you will find them now in the Basque country as we move for a while away from the sea.

Vitoria, standing at 1,800 feet, is the modest capital of the province of Alava, and is not overburdened with artistic and historic memories, though you may wish to pay your respects to the silver Virgin of the Rosary in the central chapel of the Ambulatory of the fourteenth-century cathedral, or to the city's Patron 'Virgin Blanca' in fourteenth-century San Miguel. Her festival on August 5 is the occasion for an outburst of all the heartier and noisier forms of Basque dancing, singing, weight-lifting and tree chopping. An oddity, in the Casa Consistorial, is the 'Machete Vitoriano' – the Sword of Vitoria – upon which oath is still taken by the highest civil authority upon assuming office, which carries with it the unmistakably clear indication that he may expect to be decapitated by it if he abuses his powers!

Vitoria strikes many British visitors as having something of an English look about it. This seems to me to be apparent only to the eye of the homesick beholder. True, many houses have large bow-windows, in the manner of Regency Bath, and what Wellington described as 'his scum of the earth' were in the district long enough to have made fair hair unusually common for Spain but, except for its climate, the resemblance is slight.

There is certainly nothing there less English than the food, and you could do worse (assuming that you are up-to-date on your insurance premiums) than to sample *callos* – small squares of tripe, cooked and served in the same earthenware platter, with bay leaves, garlic and slivers of red pepper plant. You had better tighten your seat belt before taking off, as I have seen this particular dish, quite literally, bring tears to the eyes of ex-Indian Army colonels who were raised on Madras curry.

After the victory of Las Navas in 1212 the little Gothic town of Gazteiz became the walled town of Vitoria, and voluntarily attached itself to the Kingdom of Castile in 1332, but was annexed by Navarre from 1366 until 1413. Near by a decisive battle was fought between Pedro the Cruel, aided by a strong British force under the Black Prince, which for a while ended the pretensions to the Throne of Castile of Henry of Trastamara, but it was not until the Napoleonic wars that Vitoria was called upon to live its finest hour.

The pattern of what the Spanish history books call their 'War of Independence' was different from anything that the French had had to compete with, at least until the 1812 Retreat from Moscow. Here, in Spain, guerrillas – and *guerra* is the Spanish word for 'war' – harassed French communications until, as one historian described it, 'the French Army was never in possession of more Spanish soil than the ground upon which it happened, at any given moment, to be standing'. One of the most brilliant *guerillero* leaders, Pedro Mina, made his base here in Vitoria – headquarters would be the wrong word for his highly secret activities. However, while Mina and his like were making life hell for any unwary group of stragglers from the French Army, preparing ambushes and dynamiting bridges, all the 'set piece' battles were fought by Wellington.

There was one such battle fought here on 21 June 1813 which gave little opportunity for brilliance since it developed into a straight slogging match between British and French troops astride the road to Manclares, within sight of Vitoria, in which each side lost between 5,000 and 6,000 men. However, when Napoleon's elder brother Joseph Bonaparte, still titular King of Spain, decided that he had had enough, Marshal Jourdain admitted defeat and abandoned 143 guns.

The pursuit of the French was, we are told, 'greatly hampered by the huge quantities of loot, much of it from Spanish

churches, which the French now abandoned'. One can easily
believe this when one gazes admiringly at the selections from
the former royal Spanish picture galleries of Madrid which today enhance the walls of the Duke of Wellington's London
residence of Apsley House!

I felt that on this journey I ought to return to the Pilgrim's
Way before approaching Burgos since, with Leon, it was the
greatest object of their devotional inspiration on their route to
Compostela, and this means only a quite short and pleasant
swing south, beside the River Ebro, by-passing Miranda de Ebro
– where so many British soldiers found their way from France
in 1940 to wait, in some discomfort, for repatriation – and if
we pause only to glimpse the wildly picturesque old houses,
walls and ruined castle of Laguardia, we soon reach Logroño,
and from there strike due west for one of the most miraculous
cities in all Spain.

If you have followed my route from San Sebastian on the
map, you may well have concluded that I have abandoned the
northern coast – Bilbao, Santander and the exciting Picos de
Europa, the cave paintings at Altamira, King Pelayo's last
stronghold at Covadonga and the strange 'rias', or firths of
Galicia. This is not so as I plan to return that way once our
pilgrimage is safely fulfilled.

5. The Pass of Roncesvalles to Burgos

As I admitted earlier, Logroño, the Roman Julia Briga, and most western city of the ancient Kingdom of Navarre – that country of wind and wild roses – is not a place where I had previously chosen to spend a night, despite its antiquity and the fact that, with nearby Haro, it grows the best table wine in Spain – I specify 'table wine' only to avoid it being compared with sherry.

However, I was delighted this time to stroll among its busy 'bodegas',* observe the remaining arch of the bridge built by San Juan de Ortega in 1138 to help the pilgrims on their way, and pay my respects to Santiago el Real – Santiago Matamoros this time – mounted upon a horse as awe-inspiring as Alexander the Great's 'Bucephalus'. Blending bodegas discreetly with churches, I took a look at the finely carved tombs in thirteenth-century San Bartolomé, and the particularly finely wrought *rejas*† in Santa Maria la Redonda, with its inspiring star vaults springing from tall shafts without capitals.

Although there is a fine 'St Francis' by El Greco in the town's 'Instituto', I had often seen its like in Toledo – El Greco, despite his greatness, seemed to repeat over and over again the same subject, as though he occasionally lacked fresh inspiration. I found Logroño's finest treasure in Santa Maria de Palacio, built in the eleventh century on a site reputedly

* Bodega : A bar, open to the public, selling only wine direct from the cask.
† Grille, often of an almost lace-like intricacy.

chosen in the fourth century by Constantine the Great.

Everyone seems to make a fuss about its slim fourteenth-century spire, known as the Needle of Logroño, being like that of Salisbury Cathedral – though why I cannot imagine, except for the seemingly universal mania for likening one thing to another instead of accepting it as it was created.

Here they hold a rather moving service, in the last minutes before the midnight which inaugurates Easter Sunday, known as the 'Kindling of the Fire'. In growing silence, one by one, all the few lit candles are put out, until there is no light except the great Paschal Candle, which is itself heavily veiled. Then at the Elevation of the Host it is unveiled and, one by one, the hundreds of candles which normally illumine the place bloom with light and, with a peal from the organ, there comes the great cry, 'Christ is Risen'.

But Logroño pales into insignificance beside Nájera, only seven miles away, not to mention neighbouring San Millán de la Cogolla, San Millán de Suso and, above all, Santo Domingo de la Calzada and the matchlessly beautiful cloisters of Santo Domingo de Silos – in short *un embarras de richesse* spread out in the quite small triangle formed by the towns of Logroño, Soria and Burgos. I am almost ashamed to say that I only now realised that I was in one of the richest centres of Reconquest ecclesiastical teaching and mediaeval pilgrimage, perhaps richer even than that surrounding Jaca.

I will not assume an equal degree of interest on your part, Gentle Reader (as Victorian novelists were apt to say), and will confine my brief descriptions to only the very best! However, to do even this, you must first know something at least of the increasingly strange setting that confronted the mediaeval pilgrim.

Very few people seem to realise that Spain is the most mountainous country in Europe, with the sole exception of Switzerland, and I must admit that, after long spells on the high, but mostly flat central plateau, I am still surprised by whole ranges far higher than Ben Nevis which I had largely forgotten! So here it came as something of a shock to be reminded that within this quite small triangle is the fierce little Sierra de la Demanda, rising to well over 7,000 feet. I expected high hills, but not considerable mountains. Perhaps one of the nicest things about Spain is that however well you think you know it, it still produces the unexpected.

I have mentioned above the great Battle of Nájera, which was fought here some 16 miles west of Logroño, but I had never previously visited the place, nor seen more than a colour photograph of Santa Maria la Real, once the pantheon of the Royal Family of Navarre (they seem to have moved their defunct monarchs about a great deal), and the scene of the crowning of the Saint–King Ferdinand in 1217. Within it today the eye is caught and held by the magnificent tomb of Blanca, Queen of King Sancho III, dating from the mid-twelfth century.

Its site was chosen by the second of the kings of Navarre as the result of an omen.

Seeing a white dove when out hawking one day he loosed his falcon to take it, and found both birds, sitting side by side in perfect amity, beneath a roadside shrine of Our Lady. However, the church he began was not consecrated until 1056, and its attractive little cloister was added as late as the sixteenth century.

More striking is San Millán de la Cogolla, first founded as a Benedictine monastery in the year 537 – nearly two centuries before the coming of the Moors – and re-built in its present form in 1554. Because of its magnificence people, inevitably, began to call it 'the Escorial of Rioja' in the tiresome way we have already noted, though it is far more charming than the slightly megalomaniac building to which they wish to liken it.

It lies in the narrow valley of the silver veins, where the precious metal was crudely mined in very ancient times, not far from Valvanera, where the image of the Patron Virgin of the whole district was discovered at the heart of an immense swarm of bees, and where there is another Benedictine abbey, famous for its library. Inside there is a great store of ninth, tenth and eleventh century incunabulae, richly illuminated with unfading blues and golds, but its greatest treasure is in the great Church Hall where, in an eleventh-century Byzantine chest, the saint's ashes now lie. His many miracles – mostly the cleansing of lepers and the restoration of sight to the blind –

are illustrated in an impressive sixteenth-century retable by Juan Rizi.

The small neighbouring chapel of San Millán de Suso is unlike any other place of Christian worship I have ever seen, not only because it is partly carved out of the living mountainside, but also because it seems almost incredible to find that extraordinary and intricate blend of Moslem and Christian architectural forms known as Mozarabic in such a wild and desolate place.

St Millán's original sarcophagus is a single, carved block of green alabaster standing near the anchorite's cave in which, it is said, he passed many years – one of many hermit's residences dotted around the area, all maintained, apparently, at sub-zero temperatures throughout the year!

By this time you will be feeling, as I was, slightly bewildered by so much concentrated magnificence, and I fear that I paid only brief respects to the Abbess Urraca Lopez de Haro in her splendid, lonely thirteenth-century tomb in the even older Chapel of Santa Maria de Cañas.

Perhaps, in addition to weariness, I was beginning to feel that it was time for something living after so much which, however beautiful it might be, belonged to so remote a past. I knew that the best of all was to be found around the former Hospice for poor pilgrims, part of which was now an almost luxurious parador for rich ones at Santo Domingo de la Calzada, and had made a reservation there for the night, so I now made the final call of a very long day at Santo Domingo de Silos.

I am eternally glad that I did, and also that I arrived there at the rather late hour when vespers were being sung by over a hundred trained male voices in Gregorian Chant.

I already knew that the monastery had been founded in the dawn of the Reconquest, but had been sacked by the terrible Almanzor of Córdoba – of whose dark deeds in Compostela itself I have written earlier – and rebuilt in 1042 in what is considered by the experts to be the climax of Romanesque art in Spain. I had also been told to make a point of seeing the silver Mozarabic chalice given by the Founder, and that, if I were benighted, even in these days, I would be given a cell in which to sleep, and food free of charge,* by the Benedictine Brothers who live out their lives there.

What I did not know was that it was the very active training place for a hundred specially chosen scholars to study and practise the disappearing art of the Gregorian Chant, nor yet anticipated the extraordinarily moving sound of a hundred deep and powerful voices raised in the disciplined majesty of this ancient style.

I stopped outside a while to listen, looking across this harsh, tawny countryside, and the centuries slid away like the memory of a troubled dream, leaving me in the heroic age when the mighty Cid and his small, devoted band of followers stormed across this same ghost-filled landscape, their rich, brocaded banners snapping in the mighty wind of their still untarnished faith.

There are places, particularly in Spain, where the veil between the centuries becomes transparent. When this occurs treasure the moment before returning to this present day of empty hopes.

When the voices inside ceased I entered the church, and later found a friendly Brother who let me spend the remaining hour of daylight alone in the cloister.

They are beyond compare in their infinitely varied beauty. Built in 1150, columns, pillars and lace-like carving are different in every case, and of an unbelievably intricate workmanship. The larger stones and panels, in high relief, describe the journey of Emmaus, and achieve an extraordinary sense of life and continuing movement. Christ himself is portrayed as a Pilgrim to Santiago, wearing his scallop shell, and after a while you begin to feel yourself a humble member of the eager, marching millions who, over the centuries, have so hopefully trodden this path.

The upper storey is in no way less beautiful, though it concerns itself with illustrating scriptural tales rather than with the pilgrimage.

---

* Lest any economically minded 'hippie' should imagine that in this ancient custom he sees the opportunity for a free holiday I should add that 'a generous contribution to the cost of upkeep is expected'. Additionally, it is strictly for men only! c.s.

In the grassy centre of the square made by the cloisters a very old cedar tree rises like a mighty admonitory finger, preserving silence, and the whole place is wrapped in an almost palpable sense of enduring peace. On the belfry stands a huge stork's nest.

I had to complete my journey to the parador at Santo Domingo de la Calzada in darkness – though the starry darkness of Spain is little more than a purple dusk – but this fitted my mood. In Spain they are used to late diners, and the parador fed and wined me superbly, but I refused to search for new impressions until I had slept a night with my quiet memories of Santo Domingo de Silos undisturbed.

Having decided to stay where I was for a second night, I made a leisurely start the next morning to explore my thirteenth-century surroundings, wandering first to the great Cathedral of Santo Domingo, begun by Alfonso III of Castile in 1148, but not finished until 1235, which is easy to recognise, not only because of its size but because of its entirely separate and detached eighteenth-century baroque belfry, which appears a trifle out of place standing close beside the very ancient little chapel of Nuestra Señora de la Plaza.

The western façade is the most picturesque, with seven orders of mouldings carried round the arch without capitals, but entering from the south gives you a dramatic, direct view of the Saint's shrine beneath the immense vault of the transept, and the huge sixteenth-century retable of wonderfully carved walnut – the last work of Damian Forment. If you enjoy wood carving at its very best, you will also find some magnificent choir stalls of the same period.

Santo Domingo was a local hermit who gave his life to helping pilgrims on their way to and from Compostela, repairing the bridge over the river Oca, and keeping the Pilgrim's Way clear and smooth for many miles in both directions. He is the saint of the road-menders, who did his humble best without any thought of winning for himself the splendours of canonisation.

Various chapels surround the fourteenth-century cloisters and, close to the door to the Chapter House, there is a monument recording the heart burial there of the usurping Henry of

Trastamara who, despite his defeat by his legitimate half-brother Pedro the Cruel assisted by the Black Prince at Nájera in 1367, lived on to rule as Enrique II from 1369 until 1379, after Pedro had been murdered in the tent of Enrique's French ally, du Guesclin.

There is much to be seen but, in one way, the Cathedral of Santo Domingo de la Calzada is unique.

On the west wall of the south transept, just above the altar, is a small room, its entrance covered by a grille, through which you may see a white cock and a black hen promenading unconcernedly, clucking or crowing to their hearts content, even while mass is being performed. Every 12 May these odd inmates are freed, and replaced by an exactly similar pair.

This strange custom goes back to the time when a father, mother and son were on their pilgrimage to Compostela but, as he was feeling unwell, the son was left behind in their lodging while the parents went to the Cathedral. Their landlady, having a taste for the handsome youth, sought to share his bed and, when he strenuously repulsed her, tore her hair and clothes, and rushed out into the street, screaming that he had attempted to rape her. (It is remarkable how often the theme of Potiphar's wife occurs, with variations, even in the most unlikely places.) By the very strict laws governing the behaviour of pilgrims, the wretched young man was forthwith hauled before the Mayor, who condemned him to immediate death by hanging.

His distracted parents, returning late, found him already hanging from the gallows, and decided that the only thing that they could do was to continue their pilgrimage to Compostela, and pray at the Saint's tomb for a miracle.

On their sad return 23 days later they found their boy still hanging on the gallows but, apparently, quite unharmed for, as he explained, St James had supported him, so that the rope could not do its fatal work, and told them that they should now go to the Mayor and tell him the truth.

However, the Mayor was just about to sit down to a splendid dinner of a roasted cock and hen, and impatiently told them to tell their story while he sat down at his table. Having heard them out he crossly replied,

'This tale that you have shewed me is as treue as if these two chekenes before mee in thys dysshe doth stonde up and dyd crowe' which, of course, they immediately did and, for good measure, flew out of the window!

For this reason the cock and hen – or rather their descendants – have been kept in the Cathedral of Santo Domingo de la Calzada throughout the last six hundred years, as a reminder and warning that Santiago will not tolerate lies and deception against those engaged in the pilgrimage to his shrine.

In addition to the Cathedral, and my own thirteenth-century parador, once known as the Hostel del Santo, there is more to see in this wonderful little city of less than 6,000 people. Chief among them is the sixteenth-century Convent of San Francisco, designed by the great Master Architect Juan de Herrera, which contains an impressive alabaster Tomb of Father Bernado de Fresnada who, as Confessor to King Philip II of Spain, had been a man of almost unlimited influence. There are also various stretches of the city's thirteenth-century defensive walls and towers still standing, and some splendid old stone houses, proudly emblazoned and still, in many cases, the homes of the descendants of their fifteenth- or sixteenth-century builders.

From whatever direction you approach Burgos your first sight of it, as it was for countless earlier pilgrims, will be of the early Gothic open-work spires rising to nearly 300 feet above the streets. When Burgos was an embattled fortress, known as 'The Shield of Castile', it had tremendous strategic importance at the indeterminate zone linking the northern *meseta*, or tableland, with the Iberian mountain network. Driving on from it in the direction of Madrid you pass through seemingly endless fields of corn, speckled with scarlet poppies – a desolate land in winter, with few signs of the many peoples who have passed this way before you, except for the painted, prehistoric Caves of Barcina, and the equally prehistoric sculpture in the Cueva de Atapuerca. Even the occasional ruined and neglected Roman amphitheatres encountered here and there seem so old as to be irrelevant. This is Old Castile, and no one has ever significantly marked its steppe-like emptiness.

But after Burgos we turn west, so we escape this almost frightening nothingness that lies at the heart of Spain.

For us Burgos is sanctuary for a while, as it was for so many millions* of earlier pilgrims – a place of peace in which to think a while and repair the damages of the long journey; to eat freshwater crayfish from the cold streams, or suckling lamb or pig – the former very much a local speciality – and savour those milk-white almonds which are so unlike the salted chips of wood which many people in Britain seem to imagine is how they should be eaten, and above all, to take our fill of the light white wine from nearby Briviseca.

But you will not be in Burgos long before you realise that this is the city of the Cid. His bearded equestrian statue dominates the main square and, San Pedro de Cardeña, just outside the town, is the place where he left his wife and young son when he was sent into exile by his vacillating, occasionally murderous king, and where both his, and his beloved Jimena's remains were buried until as late as 1921 (apart from the usual Napoleonic desecration at the beginning of last century), when they were brought in state to the great Cathedral itself, to lie, side-by-side, in eternal glory.

He has become the embodiment of the spirit of the Reconquest, but his story has been confused by thick layers of very much later poetic legend. However, unlike Don Quixote, or even King Arthur, he is known to have lived, fought and died in the eleventh century. We know, quite certainly, many of his deeds, though the bards and poets have often confused his motives, seeking to make their hero superhuman, and so unreal – as was the fashion. But a few of the facts that we do know with reasonable certainty are worth brief recall, here if anywhere.

Burgos was a dependency of the Kings of Leon until Fernan Gonzales set himself up as the first ruling Count of Castile in the year 932. His great-grandson, Ferdinand the Great, by marrying Sancha, heiress of Leon, united in himself the two most powerful Christian states in Spain during his long (by mediaeval standards) and successful reign from 1037–65.

* At the height of its popularity it is estimated that half a million pilgrims passed this way each year. C.S.

El Cid Campeador* was born Rodrigo Dias de Vivar in 1042 in a corner of the still standing Convent in the otherwise forgotten little village of Vivar de Cid, some six miles north of Burgos and, for reasons which are too complex to go into here, was taken into the household of Ferdinand the Great.

We know that Don Rodrigo could read and write, in Latin, of course, (though his spelling was somewhat uncertain), which, in those days, was comparatively rare, and he early revealed an exceptional skill in horsemanship and, above all, in the use of arms.

As the result of these accomplishments he was knighted just before his eighteenth birthday in the Church of Santiago de los Caballeros, just outside Zamora, his spurs being fastened by no less a person than the king's daughter, Doña Urraca.

These bare facts are followed by the usual kind of epic romances always attached to semi-legendary heroes – his choice of a colt that was to become his awesome war-horse 'Babieca', and what must have been half-real, half-fanciful victories over Arab 'kings' who, in fact, were little more than local Moorish chieftains. There were also various tales of how he killed his bride-to-be's father, the Count of Gomez, for having insulted his own agèd father and pillaged his lands, but these complicated tales are only for those with the time and inclination to follow the countless confusing, often directly contradictory 'romances' that were, much later, attached to his name.†

Oddly enough the great Christian paladin's first historic appearance finds him fighting against his Christian uncle, Ramiro of Aragon, in partnership with, among others, the Moorish King of Zaragoza, al-Muqtadir who, during the battle, succeeded in killing El Cid's uncle without, apparently, any protest on the part of his loving nephew!

To understand this kind of thing it is necessary to realise

---

* El Cid Campeador. *El Cid* is, roughly 'the Leader' or 'Chief' though, oddly enough, a Moorish title, and *Campeador* means 'Champion' – but the whole thing does not translate well into English. c.s.

† Anyone wishing to find their way through this maze of epic poetry is warmly recommended to Stephen Clissold's *In Search of the Cid* (Hodder & Stoughton).

that between bouts in the great 'Jehad', or Holy War, there were long periods when Moors and Christians not only co-existed but became temporary allies to acquire some real or hoped for short-term advantage against some inconvenient neighbour, be he Moslem or Christian. The more one reads of the 'protection' rackets on both sides which were general at this stage of the Reconquest, the more convinced one becomes that the late Mr Capone of Chicago was a mere amateur!

The next great milestone in the life of El Cid was when, in 1064, the ageing King Ferdinand the Great decided to arrange for the formal partition of his realms to take place after his death. He left Castile to his eldest son Sancho, with Zaragoza as his zone of future conquest; Leon and Toledo to his second son Alfonso, and to his youngest son, Garcia, Galicia and the northwest of what is today Portugal, with Badajos and Seville, respectively, as their zones of conquest. His two daughters, Urraca and Elvira, were bequeathed great convents, together with their considerable revenues. All five children had to swear to accept these arrangements with, so it is said, an added counsel that, if in difficulty, they should be guided by the advice of Don Rodrigo de Vivar who, from now on, I will refer to only as El Cid.

Ferdinand's brood were not a very savoury lot either by present-day, or even by mediaeval standards. Doña Elvira disliked the celibacy that was imposed upon her as an abbess, and was soon involved in a series of scandals, and there is plenty of evidence that Doña Urraca was dominated by an incestuous love for her brother Alfonso. Sancho was furious at his exclusion from Leon, and the story of the last years of the old king, who had achieved so much, bears an almost Lear-like sense of betrayal, tragedy and hatred. Sickened by the whole atmosphere of his court he rode off with El Cid in an unsuccessful effort to conquer the great Moslem stronghold of Valencia – a city that was to figure fatefully in his young companion's own later life. Feeling his powers slowly waning, he then returned to die in his earlier capital of Leon in 1065.

Sancho's brief reign of seven years was to see some of the greatest of all the achievements of El Cid, though their tale does not belong here. Suffice it to say that Garcia, the youngest

of the brothers, was imprisoned in the Castle of Burgos by
1071 and, after his lands had been divided up between Sancho
and Alfonso, spent 17 years in chains before released by death.

This was only a preliminary to the inevitable struggle for
supremacy between the rough and violent extrovert Sancho
and the sly Alfonso but, with El Cid helping Sancho, Alfonso
was beaten with humiliating thoroughness at the Battle of
Golpejerra and, like Garcia, was locked up in prison but, following the desperate pleadings of Doña Urraca, was released
on condition that he returned to Toledo. Once Alfonso was
safe, his sister–mistress Urraca shut herself up in the fortress of
Zamora, so strong that even the terrible Almanzor was hard
pressed to capture it.

With the remorselessness of a Greek tragedy, Sancho was
thus drawn towards Zamora and, in the dark of the night of
Sunday 7 October 1072, one Vallido Dolfus, believed to have
been a German, stole out of the beleaguered city by what is
today still called the Gate of Treachery, entered the King's
camp, found King Sancho, and struck him to the ground with a
mortal wound. Alfonso and Urraca lost no time in seizing
Burgos, and El Cid was got out of the way by assigning him to
the relatively unimportant task of collecting some overdue tribute but, urged on always by the sinister Urraca, the clash between the paladin and the fratricide–regicide king moved inexorably nearer.

To cut a long story short – or at least shorter – Alfonso's
subjects became increasingly estranged from the unnatural
pair, and the day came when, before they would acknowledge
him as their true king, Alfonso was forced to swear a public
oath that he had not been in any way concerned with his
brother's murder and, in addition, the oath had to be administered by El Cid.

To be fully binding the ceremony had to take place in front
of the Church of Santa Gadea (Agatha) in Burgos, and sworn
upon some sacred object. So it finally came about, and the dia-
logue between El Cid and the guilty king was as follows:

'Will you swear that you had no part in the ordering of King
Sancho's death?'

'I so swear.'

13   *Monastery of Las Huelgas, Burgos*

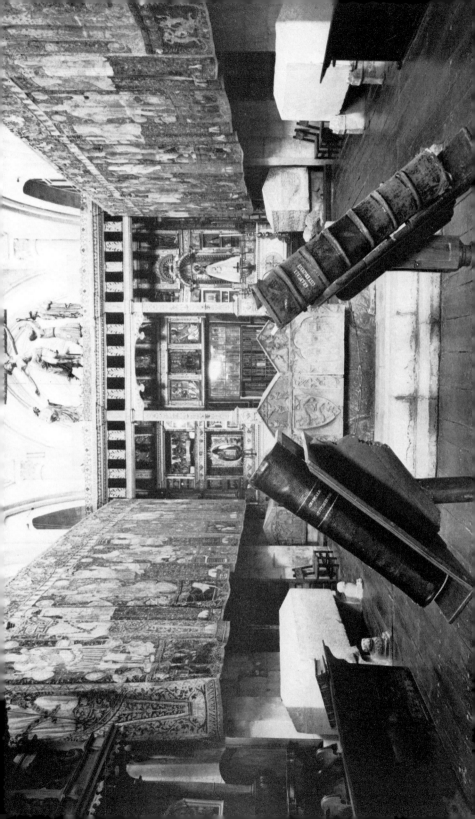

'Do you swear that you had no part by way of design in King Sancho's death?'

'I so swear it.'

'If you are foresworn, may you die such a death as your brother did, struck from behind by the hand of a traitor. Say "Amen".'

'You press me too far, Rodrigo!'

'Say "Amen".'

Although he blenched, and his voice faltered his 'Amen' set his seal to the oath, but when El Cid knelt to kiss the new King's hand in vassalage, Alfonso snatched it away, and decreed his immediate exile.

Pausing only to leave his wife and newly born son in the neighbouring Convent of San Pedro de Cardeña, today a rather grim Trappist monastery but then lovingly tended by Benedictines, El Cid rode off to his many conquests and ultimate death, in 1099, in that same Moslem stronghold of Valencia which he had once contemplated, seated beside his old patron, King Ferdinand.

Jimena clung to her dead husband's greatest conquest for years until Alfonso found the time to visit the place, and then to abandon it as something which, with El Cid gone, was beyond anyone's power to hold.

But brooding on the spirit of ancient Burgos does not excuse us from a day or two of sightseeing in the city of today, for it is still one of the fairest of all the jewels that lie along the Pilgrim's Way to Compostela – a city which did not reach its present filigree of Gothic splendour until 200 years after the birth of El Cid, when the thirteenth-century Saint–King Ferdinand changed the great Cathedral into an intricately carved mountain of pale stone.

Though the Condestable Chapel, shaped around the stone beneath which lie the remains of El Cid and Jimena,* is of a breathtaking magnificence it is, perhaps, one of the most modern things contained in this mighty 350 by 190 feet building.

Emotionally speaking, the strangest is the crucified figure of El Santo Cristo. Its miraculous appearance floating on the sea,

* Jimena is often written Ximena in old records. Both J and X are pronounced as H in Spanish anyway. c.s.

14 Burgos Cathedral, where El Cid is buried

and its equally miraculous incorruptibility, led to the belief that it was modelled by Nicodemus directly after witnessing the Crucifixion, and had been rendered indestructible by the Will of God, so that the world should possess a true likeness of His dead Son.

To me it is a little frightening, and it was only at the repeated urging of the ecclesiastic who first showed me around, many years ago, that I could bring myself to obey his urging that I should actually touch and test the skin. It is exactly the same as human skin, chill, but resilient to pressure, and possessed human hair and nails. It both sweats and bleeds freshly each Easter from the wounds inflicted by its Crown of Thorns. The rather incongruous petticoat with which the loins are covered seems to me only to increase the sense of horror inevitably inspired by a figure of such almost unbearably realistic agony.

It was found just as it is today, and as it was carried to its present place all the bells tolled, though no human hand touched the bell-ropes.

If this extraordinarily moving image stresses the darker side of Spanish Catholicism, then turn for relief to the glorious fifteenth-century stained-glass rose window, through which capricious jewels of sunlight adorn the grey granite walls and pillars, or spread strangely patterned carpets before your feet.

The central choir is sheltered by delicate wrought iron grilles, enclosing 103 marvellously carved walnut wood stalls, inlaid with boxwood, each one with its different tale to tell. The 17 separate chapels encircle the walls in a strange irregularity, varying widely in size, period and style, the oldest being the small Chapel of Saint Nicholas beyond the north transept, but each one of them offering us some unique treasure of rarest art, in silver and ivory, gold and jewels, carving and wrought iron-work looking as delicate as lace, paintings and centuries-old embroidered vestments, chalices, incunabulae dating back to the tenth century written in Visigothic lettering, and even the original marriage settlement of El Cid.

If you wander around long enough you will also come across the Cofre del Cid – the metal-bound chest which he filled with sand and pledged with the local Jews (as being filled with gold) against a loan of 600 marks. When he returned, rich with the spoils of victory, he went to repay the loan, and to confess the deception. However, when the chest was opened it was found to be full of gold, even as El Cid had said. This was a miracle in any way that you may care to regard it, though whether a divine one, or only a miracle of tact on the part of the money-lenders (who thereafter enjoyed the protection of the national hero) is one of those questions which you must decide for yourself!

You will stay as long, or as little as you wish in the cathedral, depending on your tastes, but personally I seem always to discover something new on each and every successive visit – it is so vast and varied a place that no single visit will ever reveal the full tale that it has to tell.

But for us, of course, we should cross the Leper's Bridge – now more politely called the Puente de los Malditos, or Bridge of the Accursed – to the great hostel known as the Hospital del Rey, at which pilgrims to Santiago de Compostela received 20 ounces of bread and 12 of meat with bone (or ten without bone) and 16 ounces of good, red Rioja wine – but for 48 hours only! In fact, despite its sixteenth-century plateresque main entrance, including a huge scallop shell, it is a great deal less interesting than the Convent de los Huelgas.

The Convent was founded by Alfonso III of Castile in 1187 as a Cistercian nunnery at the request of his Queen Eleanor, daughter of our Henry II and sister to Richard Coeur de Lion. Here the Saint–King Ferdinand III was knighted in 1219, and the Black Prince lodged in 1367 after the Battle of Las Navas, or Navarrete.

At first Las Huelgas was the antithesis of most austere Cistercian foundations, being the home of many queens, infantes and infantas, and the abbess was a Princess-Palatine, with absolute rule over 51 manors. Alfonso XI was crowned here in 1331, and here, too, Pedro the Cruel was born and as a child used to play in the great thirteenth-century cloisters – though, judging by his later record, one cannot help suspecting that his idea of playing consisted in pulling the wings off live butterflies – but the two kneeling figures on opposte sides of the High Altar are those of the founders, Alfonso XI and Queen Eleanor.

However, it is now a pantheon for no less than 16 royal tombs – some of them Mudejar and Romanesque – and they were all opened in 1942 or 1943 at the orders of General Franco, when a great wealth in jewels, crowns and ancient materials were found adorning the mummified bodies within.

In the centre of the nave lies King Sancho III, who reigned only for the single year of 1157–8, father of the founder, Alfonso III, whose coffin was lined with priceless Arabian cloth, covered with inscriptions. On either side of the nave are the tombs of infantes and infantas (or princes and princesses), including that of the Infante Don Fernando de la Cerda, son of Alfonso X (known as the Wise), which was one of the few not profaned by Napoleon's plundering troops, and contained articles of exceptional beauty. His mummified body was found to be wearing a light green tunic, over which was draped a rich cloak. Upon his head was set a cap of coral, gold and mother of pearl, and the inner, wooden coffin was lined with Arabian silk. One hand was crossed over his chest, and the other held a mighty broadsword. Strangely enough both his shoes had disappeared, while his spurs remained. He bore the heraldic leopards of England, and the baldric of his sword was ornamented with the insignia of his Knightly Order.

Unfortunately Don Fernando, who was the heir, died in 1275 when he was only 25, and nine years later his younger brother Sancho drove their father off the throne.

If you have the time, take a look at the Museo de Ricas Telas – I, too, am allergic to all but the briefest of visits to museums – but this is unique because it contains some of the ancient fabrics, jewellery and arms, Christian, Moorish and Oriental, taken from the royal pantheon. Behind it is a little-known Chapel de Santiago.

The grand old bridge-gate of Santa Maria, through which El Cid rode into exile, and the Casa del Cordon, where Ferdinand and Isabella received Columbus in 1496 on his return from his second voyage of discovery, may catch your eye but, in my opinion, there is only one more obligatory call before we can leave Burgos with a clear conscience, and that is to the Cartuja de Miraflores – *Cartuja* can be translated as 'Charterhouse' and *Miraflores*, rather charmingly, as 'looking at the flowers –

which was built between 1441 and 1451.

The first time I went there I had an introduction to a young monk, once rich and titled, who, after suffering a terrible loss, had taken refuge from the world in the extraordinary peace that can undoubtedly be found by those of a certain temperament by a total renunciation of the outside world.

However, my reason for coming on this occasion, and for once again crossing the simple garden patio with its three divisions (one for the public, one for the lay-brethren and the third for the silent Order of monks who are the core of the place) was to renew my memories of the fifteenth-century tomb of Juan II and Isabel of Portugal, with its 16 lions supporting the royal arms, and of their son the Infante Alfonso, brother of the great Isabella the Catholic. She would not have ruled if her young brother had not predeceased her. In fact she succeeded her elder brother, impolitely known to history as Henry the Impotent! In fact there is no evidence that he was impotent, merely that he was a homosexual – but the history books were written before the permissive age!

The Tomb of Juan II is a masterpiece, second only to that of another Juan, the only son of Ferdinand and Isabella, which may be seen at Santo Tomás just outside Avila, who died from over-indulgence in the delights of lovemaking. His likeness lies there, as though asleep, lightly smiling at the memory of the latest sweet embrace. The doctors had urged Isabella to enjoin upon him a greater continence, but the pious Queen, rather surprisingly, absolutely forbade any attempt to interfere with the pleasures of the marriage bed! If she had, perhaps Spain would have been spared the dark stain of madness which flowed from Juan's sister Juana, who succeeded Ferdinand and Isabella.

Before leaving the Cartuja de Miraflores, take a moment to look at the monks' stalls, exquisitely carved by Martin Sanchez in 1488 and, in particular, that of the officiating priest's stall, which almost defies belief in its delicate intricacy.

But it is still a long way to Compostela, and there are other pleasures of a more mundane kind to enjoy before again taking to the shadeless *meseta*. Perhaps, in parting, we can do no better than to pass through the horseshoe-shaped Gate of San

Esteban, and climb to the ruined castle that was once the home of the Counts of Castile. From there we can see, set out before us, the whole city, with the winding River Arlanzon, its heart-lifting ring of pilgrim-haunted churches, monasteries, hostels and chapels, and the gigantic Gothic forest of stone that shelters El Cid and his much-loved Jimena.

6. Burgos to Salamanca – the Unofficial Route

The road to Compostela from Burgos via Leon runs almost due west, and sometimes the actual stones of it in its primitive form are visible, like fleshless bones. But it is no road for any but the most doughty of modern cars, and unless you are a very serious and literally minded pilgrim (but still not a devout enough one to make the journey on foot) then a jeep, however out of character it may seem, is probably the most sensible method for covering this stretch!

I myself bumped along as far as Carrión de los Condes, passing on my way the ruined ninth-century castle of Castrojerez; Fromista's time-scarred twelfth-century church, and even the splendid church of the English branch of the Knights Templar at Villasirga – all of which involved me in a good deal of zig-zagging and some slight frustration, as signposts are rare – or to be more exact, tend to refer to nothing nearer than Leon or Palencia.

I found myself driving through a strange, seemingly empty world – so old that it had lost the sense of human warmth – eroded, treeless, dusty and despairing, though Carrión still raises the broken teeth of something still just living into the empty sky.

Time was when the Counts were judged rich and powerful enough to marry the two daughters of El Cid, Doña Elvira and Doña Sol but, instead of bringing them home with loving pride, they stripped them naked and whipped them, leaving them helpless and bleeding by the roadside. As might have been anticipated, they were soon made to pay very dearly indeed for their brutality to the daughters of such a father.

Once Carrión de los Condes played an heroic part as a Christian outpost against the ever-present Moslem threat, and it is well worth while to pause here before the Romanesque Church of Santa Maria del Camino (St Mary of the Road, i.e. the road to Compostela), and also to take a look at the twelfth-century Church of Santiago, where there is a frieze relating the trials and tribulations of the pilgrims in precisely this wild and bandit-infested area. All that is left of the once great Benedictine Monastery of San Zoil near by are the cloisters, where bread and wine were freely served to needy pilgrims.

However, once a year the little forgotten town comes to at least a simulation of life for its great fiesta commemorating the successful scuffle which put an end to the district's humiliating annual tribute to the Moors of a hundred virgins – a scuffle which was later 'built up' until it was dignified by the title of the Battle of Clavijo!

The whole story is depicted on the principal façade of Santa Maria del Camino, and shows a number of fighting bulls attacking the Moors, while carefully avoiding the virgins – these same Mithraistic bulls which are somehow never far distant from the mythical side of the Jacobean pilgrimage.

If you bravely persist in following the Pilgrim's Way to Sahagún you will find it a melancholy little town, once sheltered by the mightiest of all the Benedictine abbeys of Spain. Founded in 907, it was much favoured by the early Kings of Leon, who re-built and enlarged it in the twelfth century. However, it had the misfortune to be the starting point for Sir John Moore's disastrous retreat* to Coruña late in 1809, and finally crumbled away, victim of the Carlist Wars of 1835. Here it was that the spears of Charlemagne's dead warriors sprouted leaves the morning after the battle, but now there is nothing left of the gigantic building, even its ruins totally dissolved by the dusty winds of the high 'meseta'.

---

* The retreat inevitably recalled to most Englishmen by the poem forced upon them at their prep. schools beginning, 'Not a drum was heard, not a funeral note, as his corpse to the rampart we hurried', etc. C.S.

At the very moment when I was leaving Burgos the outer world of the nineteen-seventies had managed to penetrate my peaceful visit to the Middle Ages – how unwise it is always to leave an address where one may be found in case of need – so on this occasion I turned south from Carrión de los Condes to the comparative civilisation of Palencia and Valládolid for extensive cabling, telephoning and airmailing and, while there, met a very old Spanish friend with whom I had shared a strange adventure – of which more a little later – who carried me off, almost by force, to see again his magnificent university city of Salamanca. All this delayed my plans by over a week, but I faithfully returned to the Pilgrim's Way at Leon as soon as I was free.

Whatever the limitations of the friendly, sleepy old county town of Palencia, busy turning out blankets for a livelihood, I was glad to see trees again – immensely tall and graceful eucalyptus and planes. It stands besides the River Carrión, near its junction with the Pisuerga, lush-seeming as an oasis after the unsheltered Castilian plateau, and I passed an undemanding and, incidentally, remarkably inexpensive night there. Tourists pass through it, of course, but en route for somewhere more glamorous such as Burgos, Valládolid or Madrid – a fact which is reflected in the prices.

I will spare you details of its fourteenth- to sixteenth-century cathedral as we are off our intended pilgrim's route though, should you enter of your own accord, do not overlook my favourite lion and knight clock, who respectively hammer out the hours and quarter-hours with a great deal of creaky clicking and rheumatic jerking, or the El Greco of St Sebastian, though there are, of course, many other things to be seen, as there are everywhere in such places in this land of castles and cathedrals.

Although there is little to suggest the fact today, Palencia is one of the oldest cities in Spain, having been the stronghold of the Iberian Vaccaei tribe, which put up a ferocious resistance to Scipio the Great before submitting to Roman rule. Similarly, though it was, like almost everywhere else in Spain, submerged by the first incredible tidal wave of Moslem conquest in the eighth century, it came to the surface remarkably quickly, and was in Christian hands again as early as 921.

Palencia had its own university as early as 1208, and St Dominic was a student there, but it was absorbed into Spain's senior university of Salamanca in 1239. The days of its greatness passed for ever when it was heavily punished by the Emperor Charles V (that is to say King Carlos I of Spain) in 1520 for its prominent part in the Comunero* revolt.

Still it is a peaceful old town, and you can do worse than spend a while in one or another of the numerous little pavement cafés that line the arcaded Calle Mayor Principal (or its slightly more elegant Isabeline – Spanish equivalent to mid-Victorian – intersection) at the hour of the evening *paseo* – that pleasantly universal Spanish sunset custom when the entire population strolls, talks, see one another, and ensure that they themselves are duly seen.

Now that we are clear of Aragón you will see an attractive crowd, small-boned and quick, often light-haired for Spaniards, and an occasional authentic beauty with the black hair and wide green eyes that cause most masculine radars to emit unmistakable danger signals!

I was off quite early the following morning on the short run to Valládolid, seeming all the shorter, no doubt, because of my long abstention from the use of proper motor roads. Although I have visited it a dozen times *en passant* I was not there this time as a sightseer so much as in order to collect the flock of mail that I had learned in Burgos had been chasing me for most of the last fortnight, dealing with which now required most of the remainder of the day.

Valládolid is not one of my favourite Spanish cities, though it has its partisans. For my taste it suffered too much at the hands of Napoleon ever to recover its real identity as a former capital of a united Spain.

It is strange at first thought to realise that even as late as the

* Charles, born in Ghent, was a complete stranger to his Spanish subjects, and when he first arrived at the age of 17, was surrounded by a circle of Flemish noblemen to whom he gave all the most influential and profitable posts. The 'Comuneros' demanded that this should cease; that the king should not leave Spain, and that money should not be exported to Flanders. Carlos only made his seat of government in Spain finally five years later. c.s.

early seventeenth century Spain had no natural capital city in the sense that London or Paris are in their respective countries. The fragmentation of the country by the Romans – who rather favoured Tarragona – then the Goths and, finally, the Moors, who again split areas of their conquest into Emirates, plus the small Christian kingdoms fighting to liberate themselves (and frequently, equally fiercely against one another) all made centralisation almost impossible. Even when, at the end of the fifteenth century, Ferdinand and Isabella ruled over a united Spain, they were so continually on the move that the nation was, as often as not, governed from any tent in which the monarchs happened at the moment to be in residence.

This lack of a capital did not seem to bother even so powerful a monarch as Carlos I, or Charles V of the Holy Roman Empire, who was usually more concerned with affairs in Flanders, Sicily or Tunis than those of Spain, so that the need for a fixed centre of government was really only apparent in the reign of that king of civil servants, Philip II, once husband of our Tudor Mary, and bitter enemy of Elizabeth the First.

In so far as there had been a national capital it had been Burgos, but then Valládolid was selected, only to be supplanted by Madrid in 1560. But even that was not a final decision as Philip III changed back to Valládolid from 1601 until 1621, when Philip IV at last officially declared that Madrid was 'the only Royal Court of Spain'.

Although Valládolid's university dates back to the middle of the fourteenth century, and achieved considerable fame during the sixteenth, seventeenth and eighteenth centuries, it then sank to the status of one of our redbrick places of higher learning, and is no longer particularly rewarding for the casual visitor. In fact, throughout the city, you have to search for the gold among the dross since its systematic plundering by Napoleon.

The Colegio de San Gregorio is one of the earliest examples of Spanish Renaissance architecture if – as I do – you like the floridly beautiful style known as 'plateresque', with one entire façade of heraldic ornament leading up to an elaborate portal which blossoms magnificently into a kind of armorial tree!

For most people, however, Valládolid is notable for only four things. First, perhaps, as the place where Christopher Columbus died in 1506, after years of ill-health and disappointment, still clinging pathetically to the belief, against rapidly accumulating evidence to the contrary, that he had *not* discovered a new world, but only the back door to the old one – Cathay.

Secondly it is famous for the huge *pasos*, or religious polychrome statuary, carried through the streets by barefoot penitents on Feast Days – these exist throughout Spain, but those of Valládolid are remarkable for their size, artistry and, occasionally, portrayal of agony – for example the Virgin of the Seven Knives – one each for the Seven Deadly Sins. Between fiestas these remarkable 'floats' are on view in the Museo Nacionál de Escultura Religiosa.

Thirdly comes the only slightly bogus House of Cervantes, where the author of *Don Quixote* certainly lived for a while around the year 1605, but which has turned into a kind of Quixote–Cervantes Museum where, as with the relationship between Conan Doyle and Sherlock Holmes, the mythical character has become more real than its creator.

Lastly, Valládolid was the home of the very nineteenth century, very Spanish playwright José Zorilla, little known outside his own country and, perhaps, not much to the taste of Spain's postwar generation, though, with its demonstrative repentances, touch of necrophiliac religiosity, and the Love of a Good Woman Redeeming the Sinner (forgive me the capital letters, but that is the way Zorilla would have liked it) still holds a high place in the opinion of the 'over fifty' generation.

His *Don Juan Tenório* in fact still forms, or, anyway until very recently formed, an integral part in Spanish theatrical education, and there is a special Zorilla season every autumn in one or more of Madrid's leading theatres. His most famous play still jerks many a middle-aged tear, so that participation in a production has tremendous prestige value for an actor, and comparisons between the contemporary Don Juan with others of earlier years is obligatory drawing-room conversation for weeks to follow. In short, where in Britain or America the highbrows, in speaking of an actor, will ask, 'But did you see his Hamlet?' in Spain, their opposite numbers will ask, 'But did you see his Don Juan Tenório?'

On this particular visit, my work completed, it was, suitably enough, while strolling along the Paseo de Zorilla with the River Pisuerga on my left that I, quite literally, ran into Paco* Muñoz, whom I had not seen since January 1939, when I had been able to help him to escape the secret police of Barcelona, just in time to save him from what was not only a certain death, but a death which would almost certainly have been a messy one. Although I knew that he had reached France safely I had heard no more of him since, and being myself then on the fringe of being swept up into World War Two for the next six years or so, the incident would probably have slipped from my mind except for the fact that it had led me directly into two distinctly bizarre adventures in the Balkans in 1940 and 1941.

First of all, I must make it clear that Paco Muñoz was no Fascist, but his father had owned a small textile mill in Barcelona, which had enabled him to send his son to Salamanca University, where he spent his time chasing a few not too elusive brunettes.

After the Anarcho-Syndicalists had taken over all real power from the Republican Government his father had been compelled to go on paying the former workers of his factory, though the raw materials with which to operate it had long since become unobtainable – his was by no means an exceptional case – so that ultimately he had to tell them that the business was bankrupt, though through no fault of his or theirs. The Committee, or Trade Union, then took possession of the factory, but informed him that he had to continue paying all salaries from his and his wife's personal bank balances. When these, too, were exhausted there was a forced 'sale' of their home and all personal possessions, including extra clothing, and when the proceeds from this had gone the same way as the rest, he and his family found themselves penniless and in the street.

However, as 'capitalists', this was not enough, and he and Paco were arrested soon after the mother, perhaps mercifully, had died.

* 'Paco' is the diminutive of Francisco, i.e. 'Frank'.

The Republican Secret Police – oddly enough known on both the Republican and on Franco's side as the Servício de Investigación Militár, or S.I.M. – was, by this time, above the law, and affected to believe that Paco or his father had other, secret sources of wealth, which they were 'unlawfully withholding from the sovereign people' etc., etc. and employed torture. Paco's father died under 'interrogation', but he himself was 'provisionally released' – probably so that he would unwittingly betray the location of the family's non-existent wealth.

It was at this stage that he came to me for possible help in escaping, probably believing that foreign correspondents had special ways and means either for escaping, or for locally 'fixing' things. (In fact few had any such powers except, perhaps, some knowledge of just whom to bribe, and how much.)

I had known Paco only as a cheerful young extrovert, and I scarcely recognised the man he had now become and, at first, it was difficult to get him to talk about his recent experiences. However, while I was arranging for his escape (at my suggestion he spent most of the days in cinemas – although the films were three years old, and the electricity for screening them subject to continual 'cuts' – or in the British Club) bit by bit, I learned, among many other things, that police torture was always conducted under the personal direction of a wheelchair cripple – a Hungarian Jew who had received his terrible injuries as a young man at the end of World War One – whose experiments in pain, without being fanciful, seemed to be directed towards scientifically breaking down a healthy mind into something which, even in his unhappy physical condition, he could afford to despise.

His name was Carlos Conrad, and his methods were then unfamiliar to the world though, unfortunately, less so today, and a few days after the Franco troops entered Barcelona on 26 January (and before my own arrest by them) I went over the S.I.M. prison in the Via Leyetana in which he had worked, so that I could personally verify the truth of most of Paco's story. I myself saw the tiny cell, of which he had told me, in which a stone slab was tilted, so that only if the muscles of your naked body were flexed, could you avoid slowly sliding down the slope. If you slept for a moment, with the inevitable relaxation of your body muscles, you must then fall from the slab to the floor, into which were set scores of small, but razor-sharp flints. I saw, too, the devices for repeating the same question endlessly to a man in solitary confinement, hammering at the very roots of his sanity. There, too, were the devices for sudden awakenings by intolerable noise, and plunging into icy water; the illuminated, moving concentric circles to draw sleepless eyes and further exhaust a terrified brain.

But that was later. Having got Paco safely out of the country, I began to build up a fairly clear picture of this man – this Apostle of Pain – and then one day I received a warning from a friend, who worked for the S.I.M. as an *agent provocateur*, that my own life was in some danger as the result of my interest in this particular individual. This interest was known, and was unwelcome. If it continued it might prove to be fatal. Knowing the power of the S.I.M. I let the matter drop, intending to resume my enquiries after a discreet interval had elpased, but events moved far too fast, and the matter temporarily faded from my mind.

Nearly two years later, in October 1940, I was in Bucharest. The Germans were already everywhere, in the hotels, the bars, the cabarets, elbow to elbow, but everyone politely talking bad French since Rumania was still officially neutral. In fact she was just another enemy occupied country, and she already had orders from her new masters to get rid of the few English still within her borders. A force of semi-official thugs, identified with the pro-Nazi Iron Guard Party, had seized power six weeks earlier, and forced King Carol into exile. Now it was engaged in terrorist activities whereby British subjects were kidnapped and, after disappearing for several days, found on some street corner in a badly beaten-up condition. The Rumanian police, of course, professed, probably with truth, that they knew nothing about it, and it was quite obvious that no one without full diplomatic status would be able to stay in the country much longer.

For several days now I and a few others had been operating a mutual protection system, checking one another's whereabouts every four hours by telephone, so that, if one of us disappeared, the delay before the Legation got busy would at least be minimised. As a war correspondent I was naturally finding out all that I could about this terrorist activity, tracing it back, step by step, to Fabricius, the German Minister in Bucharest. Then one day the incredible happened. I discovered that Fabricius merely dictated the political lines along which the persecutions were to proceed. He gave his suggestions to a man whose headquarters were in Brașov – and his name was Karl Konradi.

Karl Konradi – Carlos Conrad – the idea suggested by the similarity of the names seemed fantastic. I immediately put into operation every line of subterranean enquiry that I possessed which, since I had been in the country for over a year, ever since I fled from Poland, were many.

Slowly the reports began to come back. No one seemed ever to have seen the man, but he was known to be a wheel-chair cripple, cruel to the point of madness in applying questions to reluctant prisoners. The former Rumanian Minister of the Interior, Marinescu, had died under his interrogation. I dropped all other work to try to follow up these clues, but conditions were becoming almost impossible, with telephone lines tapped and a permanent 'shadow' dogging my footsteps.

Late one night my telephone rang, and a voice in German said, 'You will be out of Rumania within 24 hours if you value your life.'

I replied in English that I only understood the civilised languages – English, French or Spanish. There was a short pause, and then another voice said in English :

'I should take notice of this warning if I were you,' and then, almost with a laugh, in Spanish :

'I had to warn you once before, you may remember – in Barcelona, about two years ago.' The connection then went dead.

The following day I bought two large metal bolts, and personally superintended their fixture above and below the lock on my door. My flat was on the fifth floor, and with the shutters down, could not be got at through the windows. Without telling him my full reasons, I obtained the private telephone number of one of the few 'live' members of the British Lega-

15 *Salamanca Cathedral – above the west door.* 16 *Near Tordesillas, on the road to Santiago, where the Knights of Santiago patrolled to protect pilgrims from robber bands*

tion, who promised to come in haste, together with one or two Rumanian policemen, armed with all the weapons of aggressive diplomacy, if I phoned him that anyone was trying to force their way into my flat.

The following day I telephoned a full story on Karl Konradi on whom I had collected many more facts, including his position in the German S.S. Both Rome and Berlin radio announced that I had fled the country. I countered this with a follow-up story, also from Bucharest – but I knew that time was running out.

Seventy-two hours after my conversation with Konradi, at 3.30 a.m. there was a ring at my flat door. Without turning on the lights I went to the door and peered through the tiny spyhole with which most continental doors were equipped. Outside on the landing I could dimly see three figures in black mackintoshes. I went to the telephone to call my Legation friend. The line was dead – cut. There was no one to whom I could shout from the window for help, as there was a rigid curfew until dawn.

In a chair facing the door I watched and listened for fully two hours as fragments of wood were prized away. Occasionally I could hear a low-voiced consultation, and then some new part of the door would be attacked, stealthily – as the outward seeming of Rumania being a neutral country had at all costs still to be observed – but with a terrifying persistence.

After a couple of hours, with occasional and increasingly frequent pauses for discussion which I could not overhear, they gave it up – though by this time the lock and one bolt had been forced – but perhaps they were convinced that the door, though weakened, could not be completely broken down without the noise rousing the whole block of flats. More probably my complete silence, and the absence of light from within, led them to believe that I was not there but, whatever the reason, as the window frames began to show grey outlines, they quietly left.

Half an hour later I switched on the lights, went into the bathroom and was extremely sick. My face in the mirror was as grey as the reluctant, blessèd dawn outside. That afternoon I was on a plane to Sofia and, very temporarily, safety.

17   *Unchanging Spain – La Alberga, Salamanca*

I had hit Konradi* on his most sensitive points – publicity, and the possibility that he might be insane – and my newspaper and the BBC gave him front-page treatment for 48 hours. For this he never forgave me. I was condemned to death *in absentia* by the Iron Guard,† and five months later, in March 1941, when the Germans were already moving into the north of Bulgaria, he made a last attempt, foiled again only by the equivocal state of peace that existed for a few more hours between Britain on the one hand and Bulgaria on the other, plus the fact that I had armed myself with a high American Legation Official (the U.S. still being neutral) and a Turkish diplomatic courier as observers!

We held up the Orient Express for three long hours, while I absolutely refused to get off that once-famous train and enter into the blacked-out frontier station of Svilingrad – and disappear. However, as I said earlier, I have no excuse for inflicting my autobiography upon you when on a pilgrimage to Santiago de Compostela! My excuse for including the incident is to explain why I could not now refuse Paco Muñoz's urgent invitation to come as his guest to Salamanca – we had much to tell one another that we could learn from no one else.

However, I only agreed to meet him in Salamanca 36 hours later, as he was attending some kind of celebration, similar to an Oxford 'gaudy', to which men of the same years at the university are invited (a mistaken form of human activity, as everyone except oneself has changed so markedly for the worse!) and I had a few places, more or less along the way, that I wished to see, so I waved him off the following morning with a promise of re-meeting the following evening.

My way was the same as his, southwest from Valládolid as far as Tordesillas but, after that, I was, as usual, bound on slightly more devious routes. It was a lovely morning as I set out for the moated castle at Simancas, where once stood the

---

* He died, much honoured by his disciples, in his native Budapest in 1957.

† The Iron Guardist entrusted with my 'liquidation' still lives in Madrid. I met him at an Embassy party some years after the event, he admitted it, and I invited him to have a drink with me the following day to celebrate his inefficiency – but he seemed a little nervous of my intentions! c.s.

Roman town of Septimanca, a castle which, in 1545, became the storehouse for the official archives of the nation. With the requisite pass, historians can there pore over an enormous mass of state documents accumulated from both before and after that year, but it is a daunting task, as they are written principally in dog Latin – and a distinctly Spanish dog at that!

Here we are still on the mainly flat meseta of Old Castile, and on the plain below the castle Ramiro II of Leon roundly defeated the Moors in the year 934, in one of the earliest significant battles of the Reconquest.

Tordesillas, some 20 miles from Valládolid, possesses an *albergue* – that is, a simplified version of a parador, specialising in meals for transients but also possessing simple sleeping accommodation which is always clean and inexpensive – standing near the strange-looking sixteenth-century bridge over the infant River Duero. Here it is only a modest stream, very different from its later self, when it flows through the deep and often swelteringly hot gorges beneath the terraced slopes where grow the grapes destined to become port wine, and which finds its final escape to the sea below the ancient Portuguese city of Oporto.

Tordesillas is completely dominated by the great Mudejar-style fourteenth-century Convent of Santa Clara, once a palace belonging to Pedro the Cruel, but far more famous as the place of confinement for no less than 49 years of Queen Juana, when, after forcible separation from her husband's already corrupting body, her jealous mania finally broke down into screaming, irremediable madness. Her now widowed, but still incurably ambitious father Ferdinand, was by no means reluctant to repossess himself of the power passed by his dead wife, Isabella, to their daughter, adopting the rôle of Regent for his infant grandson Carlos for the next ten years. Carlos, as elected Emperor of the Holy Roman Empire, King of Spain, the Netherlands and Sicily, was to become a dominant personality in world power politics during the first half of the sixteenth century.

Poor Juana la Loca – Joan the Mad – spent nearly half a century in strictest confinement here, dying, in 1555, only three years before her famous son, and only one before he retired from the world to the Monastery of Yuste, where he spent much of his remaining time attending dress rehearsals of his own funeral! Juana left a dark shadow over both her son and her grandson, Philip II, which took the form of progressive religious mania.

It is said that, of choice, she lived most of her time in the total darkness of a single, windowless cell, though in 1520 the Comuneros sought to use her against her son, but she was sane – or lucky – enough to refuse.

Although primarily known as the prison of Juana la Loca, the Convent dates back for nearly two centuries before her tragic tale, and it was here that the representatives of Spain, Portugal and the Borgia Pope Alexander VI met in 1494 to rectify their earlier decree on the division of the still largely undiscovered New World – an error, so it is said, made on the earlier occasion by the cartographer Amerigo Vespucci. It is this meeting at Tordesillas so long ago which is responsible for the fact that the people of Brazil today speak Portuguese, and those of Central, and the rest of South America, speak Spanish.

Without a special permit visitors may only visit the Church of the Convent of Santa Clara which, if you admire Mudejar architecture, is well worth doing, so I was soon on my way south to Medina del Campo – the City of the Plain – where, between September fifth and eighth, a *toston* of pork, roasted in the open in the main square, is offered to all prepared to eat it on the spot. This involves you in scorching your lips and fingers, and decorating your clothes with grease – unless you come prepared. With it are provided considerable quantities of pleasant, dry red wine – also free!

Medina del Campo is not a place which appears to have much to offer, except for its reputation for being the centre of the richest wheat-growing area in all Castile but, as so often in Spain, a little inquisitiveness is rewarding.

The fourteenth-century collegiate church of San Antolin contains the personal banner of the Catholic Kings, the high altar shows the master-hand of Berruguete, and there is a pleasantly surprising baroque Chapel. Santiago has his church to remind us that we are not so very far from his great road to Compostela, and San Martin gives another glimpse of Mudejar.

Additionally, too, there are some splendid, escutcheoned, six-teenth-century private mansions – the Casa de las Duenas being perhaps the noblest.

However, Medina del Campo is famous first and foremost as the place where the incredible, red-headed, green-eyed Isabella died, still only in her early fifties, in 1504, worn out by her demon-driven efforts to be a great queen – in which she most certainly succeeded – and a good mother. As a mother she was less successful owing to the fact that most of her pregnancies were passed tearing from one point of danger to another on horseback over unspeakable roads!

The Castillo de la Mota, with its bartizan turrets, about a mile outside the town, was built by Isabella's father Juan II in 1440, and from 1504–6 it was the prison of Cesare Borgia, the brilliant son of Pope Alexander VI, held here in the closest confinement at the most urgent request of Alexander's successor, Pope Julius II. Cesare's luck was mysteriously bound up with that of his wicked old father, and once a jeering Roman crowd had crammed him into a very small coffin, and convinced themselves that this death was genuine, and not like his earlier one – a trick to discover just who were his real enemies – then Cesare's fortune utterly deserted him. He escaped from the Castillo de la Mota after two years at the price of breaking both his hands and wrists in his leap for liberty.

There was a palace close beside the Castillo, now a meaningless ruin, which is almost certainly the place where Isabella died – sternly forbidding her doctors and their assistants to raise her skirts to secure a more certain diagnosis since this, she remonstrated, would be improper!

Arévalo, where Isabella was baptised, was my next objective, on what was still, by my standards, a good road and, as I approached it, I could clearly see the towers and bastions of the Sierra de Guadarrama to the southeast and, very faint against the empty, pale sky, a finger tracing of shadow that was the Sierra de Gredos, far to the southwest. After so much bone dust from the ancient meseta my heart sang with the words 'the hills, from whence cometh my help'.

Arévalo, though rarely visited by tourists, is a sturdy little town, full of strong sixteenth-century stone houses. Its Church of San Salvador claims to be founded on a site selected by Constantine the Great in the fourth century. While this could perhaps be no more than pious legend, the neighbouring Convent of San Francisco was certainly founded by that greatest of the latterday Saints, St Francis of Assisi in 1214 (though in honour of St Bernard), and here St Francisco de Borja – of the same family, though of distinctly different habits, as the profligate Borgia Pope Alexander VI – lived for several years.

Here, in little known Arévalo, stands Santa Maria, with its high, towered gate – the Arco de Santa Maria – which once formed part of the city's defensive walls: twin-towered San Martin, equipped with arrow-slits, should the occasion demand action rather than peaceful prayer, and the Castle of the Convent of San Bernardo el Real beside the River Ádaga. A mile to the south are the ruins of the Cistercian nunnery of Nuestra Señora de la Lugareja – one of the land's most beautiful examples of brick Romanesque, dating from the thirteenth century.

It was a surprise, when, in poking my nose into the lovely old Casa de las Cadenas, I found myself confronted by a carved stone bull which had somehow found its way to this remote place all the way from Carthage or, more probably, been created by the orders of Hannibal when he passed this way in 219 B.C. No one seemed to be able to tell me much about him – though bulls ancient and modern tend to crop up all over the place in Spain. Perhaps he was a small brother of the three giant bulls of Guisando which lie, untended, in a stony field no great distance from Ávila, looking more like hippopotami than bulls but, like the smaller one with which I was now confronted – all old, very old, long before the arrival of the Romans.

Had I continued by the same road I should have left the dusty uplands and climbed through the insanely rock-strewn passes to the perfect eleventh-century walls of Ávila, birthplace of that doughty old suffragette of a Saint, Teresa, who stood no nonsense from anyone – not even from God if He was making life unnecessarily difficult!* Had that been possible I

---

* A pleasant story of Santa Teresa records her extreme displeasure at the fact that no sooner had she knelt to pray than divine levitation began,

should have continued south and then east into the Sierra de Gredos, where so many times I have combined the pleasures of dreaming dreams with the catching of numbers of delicious trout from the infant River Tormes.

But this time my way lay due west from Arévalo on a side-road to Madrigal de las Altas Torres – the Song of High Towers or, if you like it even better, The Love Song of High Towers – where I had booked myself into the modest local parador for a night.

Madrigal de las Altas Torres – surely the most enchanting name for so old, and oft forgotten a little town – is where Isabella was born to King Juan II and Queen Maria of Aragón in 1451. Juan was married again to Isabella of Portugal, so that the great Queen to be had a lonely childhood, except for her younger brother Alfonso, who was to predecease her, while her mother showed early signs of mental decay.

Even in her late teens Isabella's chances of achieving the powers she alone instinctively knew how to wield must have looked extraordinarily slim.

A descendant of a rotting royal line, with a still young homosexual half-brother on the throne as Henry IV, whose Queen, Juana of Portugal, was determined to foist her girl bastard by the great Knight Beltran upon the nation after her lord and master's premature demise. (Beltran, by the way, served his king similarly and, apparently, equally satisfactorily as he served his queen.) Lastly, Isabella must give precedence to her own much-loved younger brother, Alfonso.

But she had powerful, and occasionally ruthless friends – mostly among the more exalted hierarchy of the Church. In any case she survived both her brother and her half-brother, and the nation – encouraged, perhaps, by those same powerful friends – ensured that the people of Castile would not accept

---

and she would often find herself floating ten feet or so above the heads of the rest of the congregation, making it necessary for her to ask the Almighty, quite sharply on occasions, to let her down to ground level. The whole business, she clearly felt, was altogether too exhibitionist, in fact slightly 'bad form'. As she lived as late as our own Queen Elizabeth the First, it is difficult to discount the many contemporary records of these strange happenings. c.s.

'La Beltraneja', as the Queen's bastard was known because of her resemblance to her famous father so, despite the odds, Isabella was Queen of Castile at the age of 23, with a 30-year reign before her.

She then had to marry the sly, unfaithful Ferdinand so as to unite her portion of Castile and Leon with his of Aragon and Catalonia, and then, finally, lash a tired and impoverished nation, and a cautious, slow-moving husband, to the final agony of effort needed to expel Spain's last Moors from the mainland.

That, despite all this, she managed to find the means that made it possible for Columbus to discover the New World was, in a way, just an accident of history so late as the end of the fifteenth century – the Portuguese, at least, were already sniffing uncomfortably close to his heels – but her gift of unity and pride of nationhood were her gift, and hers alone.

The walls of Madrigal de las Altas Torres today are ruinous, but their form is unusual in that they are a perfect circle about a mile in circumference, and are pierced by four great armed gates facing precisely north, south, east and west – the *altas torres*, or high, fortified towers which gave the place its name. Of these the west gate – the Puerta de Cantalapiedra – is the only one to have survived both war and weather almost undamaged.

Today Santa Maria del Castillo is a rather baffling collection of buildings. First, on the site of a Moorish mosque there is – decidedly late for its architectural style – a seventeenth-century Romanesque church, to which a baroque retable, with a singularly beautiful custodia, was added. But it is in the Hospital Real, founded in 1443 – exactly eight years before Isabella's birth – that you enter what remains of the little palace.

Public entrance is obtainable to the Chapel Royal, with its beautifully broad, unsupported arched roof, and its macabre, but moving thirteenth-century Cristo de las Injurias. The rest of the former palace is the home of 24 impoverished Sisters of the Closed Order of St Augustine, and I had had to obtain a most imposing special pass from their Bishop before I was allowed inside, and even then my stay was distinguished by its speed rather than by its dignity!

After a glimpse of the charming little patio I was preceded by the priest–confessor of the sisterhood, ringing an outsize handbell – the variety favoured by Lord Hailsham some decades ago – presumably to scare away any absent-minded or (might I still hope?) curious nun, unaware of the rapidly approaching Horror of Dracula which, somehow or other had been let loose to destroy their serenity. For this reason I made my visit as brief as possible, though there was much more I would have liked to see, and, still more, to have asked.

My chief impression was of lovely, almost empty rooms, with high, carved ceilings, genuine fifteenth–sixteenth-century furniture and wonderfully bright, alive-seeming frescoes – perhaps the first, misty vision of the girl-child born here nearly five and a half centuries ago to such a mighty destiny.

I was told that on Good Friday the stairs leading to the alcove in which Isabella was born must be mounted upon their knees, with an appropriate prayer at each pause, by every resident of the community. No one seemed quite sure why this rule was observed, and to me it smacked a little of idolatry since – though her position as a national heroine is firmly established – Isabella has never been canonised.

The financial foundation of this little community was emphatically not over-generous, despite the fact that it provided the royal family with such a convenient place for the disposal of their female bastards. However, Philip II freely acknowledged a certain Doña Ana as being his niece, since she was unquestionably a natural grand-daughter of his father Charles V.

There is a little-known incident centred around this pale and ghostly home for unwanted semi-royals.

Don Juan of Austria, illegitimate son of Charles V by Barbara Blomberg, was born in Ratisbon in 1547 and, when he himself was only 21, had an affair with the aristocratic Maria de Mendoza resulting in a daughter who, after being christened Ana, was hustled off into the care of Doña Magdalena de Ulloa *'para no dar motivo de disgusto a Felipe'*.*

At the age of 16 she was placed in the Convent of the Augustinian Sisters in Madrigal de las Altas Torres. This was in 1584 – six years after her father's premature death in Flanders

* Trans. 'so as not to give grounds for displeasure to Philip II'.

and four after her uncle Philip II had taken possession of Portugal. The King had been kept ignorant of Ana's existence until after Don Juan's death, but when he heard of it he permitted her to take the name of Ana of Austria, together with a pension and other privileges, though he refused the son of the Duke of Alba's plea for her hand in marriage.

All had been handled without undue scandal according to the fashion of the times, but after ten years in a convent the 26-year-old and very beautiful Ana was ripe for trouble.

It came in the rather unlikely person of a 50-year-old gentleman, Don Gabriel de Espinosa, who arrived in Valládolid in 1594, where he was at some pains to hint that he was not of the humble origins he appeared, and was even so unwise as to produce a jewelled miniature of Ana of Austria, saying that 'although a nun she could marry if she wished, since she had protested at the time that she entered the cloister against her will'.

Next a prostitute, whose house he frequented in Madrigal, noticed that Don Gabriel possessed a very large sum in gold secured to his person which, fearing that it might be stolen money which would implicate her if the theft came to light, she reported to the *alcalde*.* He sent two *aguaciles*† to arrest him for interrogation, but they found that Don Gabriel was not at his lodgings, and learned that he rarely stayed two nights running in the same place – an additionally suspicious circumstance – but they finally tracked him down at about 2 a.m. in a low *posada*‡ and finding him in bed ordered him to dress and accompany them. They noticed, we are told, that his linen was remarkably fine, and that the collar and cuffs of his point lace were fastened (not detachable for washing) in the manner affected by the rich.

The room was searched, disclosing gifts from the royal family – one from the King himself – which had been sent to Ana of Austria, the King's niece, which Gabriel volunteered

---

* *Alcalde*. Today simply the mayor but in old times possessing the powers of an examining magistrate.

† *Aguaciles*. More or less policemen, but acting only on instructions from the alcalde.

‡ *Posada*. A doss-house – at least in the sixteenth century.

had been entrusted to him by her for sale. Brought before the alcalde he stated that he was a pastry-cook, and then tried to carry off the situation by blustering that the 'alcalde might find himself in trouble with high personages' if he meddled in the matter. Understandably the alcalde, nevertheless, clapped him into gaol pending further enquiries!

In Madrigal the aguaciles the next day found a large packet of letters, two of them from a Portuguese Augustinian Friar named Miguel dos Santos, confessor to the nuns of the convent, and a man, moreover, who had been in serious trouble 14 years earlier for his opposition to the Spanish occupation of Portugal in 1580. He had also once been chaplain to King Sebastian I of Portugal, who had perished, or at any rate disappeared, at the disastrous Battle of Alcazar-el Kabir in 1578 in his half-insane crusade against the Moors – a death or disappearance which alone had lent some appearance of legality to Philip II's seizure of the country in the rôle of Sebastian's uncle.

Another two letters were from Ana of Austria to Gabriel de Espinosa, couched in passionate terms of affection, but referring to him as 'Your Majesty'. The alcalde decided that this 'pastry-cook' was a problem upon which only King Philip could decide, and sent the whole dossier on to him, while retaining Don Gabriel safe under lock and key.

Philip realised quite quickly that the plot was for Ana and Gabriel to marry; to smuggle themselves into Portugal, and then to declare that 'Gabriel' was the vanished King Sebastian* for whom the country was longing as an alternative to Spanish occupation.

He immediately despatched his personal almoner, Don Llano Valdes (with special privileges from the Papal Nuncio to permit him, if necessary, to use torture on the dubious Friar Miguel dos Santos) with orders to uncover the whole story.

Both Gabriel and dos Santos were questioned under torture, but always retracted what they had said in their moments of

---

* There was a cult of 'Sebastianism' prevalent in Portugal at this time, and there had been various claimants to be the missing monarch. Professor Livermore discusses the cult fully in his *History of Portugal*, and I have touched on the subject in my *Introducing Portugal* (Methuen, 1956) and again in my *Portugal* (Batsford, 1970).

delirious agony. In 1595 the sentences were promulgated, and their severity was proof of Philip's conviction that they were engaged in an attempt to restore the Portuguese monarchy and, possibly, of his belief that Don Gabriel might genuinely have been the lost King Sebastian. Of that we shall never be certain.

Ana was condemned to strict seclusion for eight years, deprived of her servants and attendants, incapacitated from ever being the head of a religious community and to fast on bread and water only on every Friday. Fortunately for her Philip II died three years later; Philip III took pity on her, and she was made perpetual Abbess of the great Benedictine nunnery of Las Huelgas near Burgos.

Friar Miguel dos Santos was led in ignominy through the streets of Madrid and hanged in the Plaza Mayor, while Gabriel de Espinosa (or King Sebastian of Portugal and Philip's nephew) was hanged, drawn and quartered in the main square of Madrigal de los Altas Torres, and his head stuck on a stake.*

However, by now Lord Hailsham's handbell was beginning to trouble my nerves as much as it was no doubt troubling the nuns whose privacy I had disturbed. All that I could do was to glimpse the chapel floor of lovely Talavera tiles, insist upon stuffing the alms-box with enough money to give the good sisters at least one substantial improvement upon their usual daily diet of thin, self-grown cabbage soup, and with the handbell still pealing (should I also have proclaimed 'Unclean, Unclean' in the best mediaeval leper tradition?) hide in the non-Women's Lib. atmosphere of San Nicolas de Bari.

Naturally, everything in Madrigal de las Altas Torres is emotionally overshadowed by Santa Maria del Castillo, but you should also pay your respects briefly to the Capilla Dorada, guarding its great carven tombs. In any case the whole town is a 'Love Song of High Towers', and I almost regretted my appointment with Paco. But regret soon vanished when once again I paused on the Roman part of the 26-arched bridge, and saw the red-gold magnificence of Salamanca reflected in the clear waters of the River Tormes.

---

* For the story of the Pastry-Cook of Madrigal I enthusiastically recommend Sir Charles Petrie's *Don Juan of Austria* (Eyre & Spottiswoode, 1967.)

7. From Salamanca to Leon

Entering Salamanca by the Roman bridge over the River Tormes almost the first major building that you will see on your left is the twelfth-century church of Santiago, which I took for a sign that, by wandering so far south from the straight and narrow way to Compostela, I had not strayed beyond reasonable forgiveness.

But I was anxious not to be tempted into too much sightseeing on my own, as I had half-promised Paco the honours of host in 'his' Alma Mater, and made my way firmly to the café of which he had given me the name in the unmistakable and magnificent eighteenth-century arcaded square known as the Plaza Mayor – one of the few relatively 'new' things in this ancient city – a vast expanse, bright with sunshine and pigeons. Bullfights were held here as recently as 1863.

I was a full hour early for our *cita** (and I have never yet known a Spaniard to be early for an appointment, which is considered 'not quite the thing' among his compatriots anyway, smacking of harassment) and this suited me well, since it not only enabled me time to reinforce myself with a couple of *copitas* before getting swept up into what I knew to be Paco's idea of a jollification, but also a chance to recall and sort out what I already knew of Spain's senior university.

Although its origins are of great antiquity the city as we see it today – even its oldest buildings – had to be re-created in the late eleventh century, so desperately had it and all the sur-

* *Cita* = appointment, engagement, rendezvous.

rounding country suffered during the fiercest period of the Reconquest, when El Cid and Ferdinand the Great were first
blunting and then, finally, turning the great Moorish Almora-
vide re-invasion. Today, once again, its glory is fading – though
in a very much less dramatic way.

Salamantica was an Iberian city of some importance when it
was captured by Hannibal in 217 B.C., and under the Romans
its name was only slightly changed to become that which it
bears today. Then it was the main staging post, and fortress
town on the Via Lata between Mérida and Zaragoza, and its
prosperity increased under the Goths. It fell, as it must then
have seemed that the whole world was falling, beneath the
fury of the first Moslem wave of conquest in the century immediately following that in which the Prophet lived, and was
not liberated until 1055. Ferdinand's second son Alfonso – he
of the incestuous sister – found that the entire country between the Rivers Douro and Tagus had become little but an
uninhabited wilderness, but it was not until 30 years later that
he gifted the ghost town to his sister and brother-in-law, Count
Raymond of Burgundy, with special grants to effect its re-
habilitation.

The 'Salamantines' as they were called were, therefore, an
understandably mixed and disorderly crew to begin with, but
in 1220 – ten years before the Kingdoms of Leon and Asturias
were united with that of Castile by the Saint–King Ferdinand –
its university was founded and, absorbing the fledgling institu-
tion created in Palencia a few years earlier, became the foremost in Spain.

However, the local temperament did not seem to have
changed a great deal, and the city had to be severely spanked
by Carlos V in 1521 for joining the Comuneros, of whose supposed or real grievances we have written above, but was officially taken back into royal favour when Carlos' son and heir,
Philip, was married there in 1543 to Juana of Portugal. The
University was officially acknowledged by Pope Alexander IV
as early as 1255, and so can fairly claim to be in the same
league as Bologna, Oxford and Paris.

This is no place to go into the gradual decay which over-
came the great university during the next few centuries, but

the fact remains that, despite its 25 colleges, today there are
barely 1,000 new undergraduates, or students going up each
year whereas, in the days of its greatness, there were 12,000.
Suffice it to say that this decline has nothing to do with the
circumstances which have so changed the whole atmosphere
of our own Welfare State Universities, but rather to peculiarly
Spanish manifestations which, in brief, may be called the ultra-
clericalism of the eighteenth and nineteenth centuries, when
the Holy Inquisition was still powerful. By that time the Inquisition had renounced burning people over niceties in doc-
trine, but it was still interfering a great deal too much with
everyone's freedom of thought.

Physically the southwestern quarter of Salamanca suffered
terribly at the hands of Napoleon's Marshal Marmont in 1811,
when he decided to make use of it as a gigantic defensive barrier against Wellington though, in fact, when Wellington returned the following year, the only military action took place
some four miles away and lasted only 45 minutes. They were
45 minutes so decisive that they led inexorably to the Napoleonic expulsion from the entire Iberian Peninsula, and the
British advance to Toulouse.

Salamanca stands high, 2,600-odd feet above the distant sea
and, as a result, knows both pitiless winter cold and blinding
summer heat, and it breeds what are supposed to be Spain's
finest fighting bulls – a fact which, while there, you will rarely
be allowed to forget!

Salamanca, like most continental universities, would probably strike a postwar English graduate as less strange than it
would one with memories of pre-1939 Oxford, when the latter
was not so much a place in which to learn as an introduction
to a way of life – unfortunately a way of life which was about
to disappear. Although there had always been Scholarships and
Exhibitions in the senior British universities, and a few hundred dedicated souls destined to become schoolmasters or
clergymen, 'student grants' were unknown, and the embryonic
'technocrats' went to Edinburgh or London. The rest were 'up'
to enjoy themselves and to learn how to enjoy other people,
and perfectly content to go down after three, or even four
years with a 'Pass' degree in some financially useless subject,

such as History or English Literature.

There was, of course, the Union for those who wanted to go into politics – but even in the Union wit was usually valued more highly than profundity. The idea that the even course of university life should be disturbed by 'Student Demonstrations' was quite unimaginable – if you did not like things as they were and always had been you either went down, or were sent down. However, on the Continent, even here in Salamanca, politics loomed far larger than in Great Britain.

But though the manner is different, the place is equally old, and as I knew that Paco's sightseeing would consist principally in introducing me to a few convivial contemporaries, and then stunning my taste-buds and duodenum into temporary submission with vast meals, I decided after all to sneak off for a private 'refresher' in Salamanca's two cathedrals.

I do not say that there are none, but I cannot personally recall another city with *two* cathedrals, of the same sect, that is. Naturally there is St Paul's and Westminster in London, but then one is Anglican and the other Catholic. *Both* Salamanca's are Catholic, and they are practically next door to each other.

Seeing that I had time in hand (and leaving a message with a friendly old waiter for Paco – just in case) I made for the Old Cathedral – the Old dating from twelfth century, and the 'New' from the sixteenth.

I made now for the Old Cathedral to look at a purely personal favourite object which it contains – namely its organ, which dates from 1342 (its pipes are held in place by Moorish tracery), which I think must be the oldest still functioning instrument of its kind in existence today. For years I have had a secret passion to play it for a few moments, since it is well over 200 years older than any other I have ever been able to approach to date. I have only once heard it played, and even then briefly, and the sweetness of its tone has always remained clear in my memory. But my, perhaps, rather childish ambition seems likely to remain unfulfilled. I was glad, at least, to see that it was still there.

Oddly enough, the Chapel of Santa Barbara in the Old Cathedral was the place where degrees were presented to those to whom they had been awarded right up until 1842 – perhaps

18 *The castle
of the
Keeper of
the City
Gates of
Salamanca*

19 *The Roman bridge and the Cathedral at Salamanca*

20   *A corner of the royal pantheon of the Kings of Leon and Asturias, including the tomb of St Isidro*

another hint of that excessive clericalism which gradually sapped the university's vitality. Incidentally, the Talavera Chapel in the Old Cathedral is one of the very few places where, very occasionally, mass is said according to the Mozarabic Rite.

It is a strange old building, warm with enduring faith and, to be more practical, is probably the most interesting Romanesque building in Spain. It is nice to think that it was begun by El Cid's Chaplain, Don Jeronimo de Périgueux. All interior decoration pales before the tremendous reredos depicting the Apocalypse – the call to the Last Judgement of the living and the dead – though your eyes may well be drawn away in fascination by the ribbed vault of the great dome in two tiers of arcaded lights, strongly suggestive of a direct Byzantine influence upon the architect.

To a superficial glance the New Cathedral is even more impressive than the Old one.

Begun as early as 1512, in the golden century of conquest and discovery, and despite the torrent of wealth that soon poured into Spain from the despoilment of the Aztec and Inca civilizations, there was still never enough to spare for all the megalomaniac projects that Charles V and Philip II sought to achieve. Philip III's reign was literate rather than architectural in its heritage so, except for the artistic afterglow left to us by Velasquez's rendering of the Court of Philip IV, there was nothing more to come from the once great Spanish Hapsburg line but poor Carlos II, drooling from his fantastically ill-fitting jaw, and doomed to die of senility at the age of 40 in financial destitution.

Everyone familiar with Spain will recognise a *madrilleno* by the fact that he lisps: few realise that this stems from the servility of Carlos II's Court, where everyone who was anyone strove to speak in the only way in which their unfortunate monarch was able to express himself. In Carlos, Juana la Loca collected the last coin of her awful debt, and the lonely, half-mad creature who was her direct descendant, loved nothing so well as to have the tombs of his mighty forebears opened, so that he could confide his insuperable problems to them, and weep over their crumbling remains.

The death of Carlos in 1700 was followed by the War of the Spanish Succession, in which most of Europe, including Britain, fought to prevent the dangerous imbalance of a Bourbon ruler on both sides of the Pyrenees. But while Marlborough and Prince Eugène finally defeated Louis XIV in France, his grandson, Philip V, somehow hung on in Spain – this was the period of Britain's acquisition of Gibraltar – but this series of disasters had, as one of its many very minor consequences, the fact that Salamanca's New Cathedral, begun so hopefully in 1512, did not receive its final touches until 1755.

Despite all these delays, it is enormously impressive, first of all because of its sheer size – 340 feet long by 160 wide – with beautifully moulded piers and a pierced balustrade, and when you begin to browse, there is a mass of fascinating detail.

The central choir is formed of elaborate tracery, all richly pictorial – saints, 'putti', arabesques and a lovely musicians' gallery in the Capilla Dorada. If you have keen eyes you will also find, rather unexpected, half-hidden hunting scenes and animals carved and painted also, along the cornices leading up to the famous 'Santa Ana and the Virgin' of Juan de Juni. Suddenly Titian's 'Entombment' blazes sombrely, and your eye later is caught by the 'Holy Family' of Morales.

But the entry to the sacristy, bright with Venetian mirrors, brings you to the building's greatest treasure – a small Byzantine crucifix made of humble bronze, but carried by El Cid with him in all his many battles. Still, if bronze seems humble for El Cid, you may see the plain wooden one which Salamanca's first Bishop used to raise on high to exhort the followers of the Christian paladin on the very field of those same battles.

Time was, by now, really short, even by Spanish standards, and I turned aside only to take a brief, grateful look at the enchanting Puerta de Ramos – the entrance portal which is most marvellously carved in relief to tell the story of Christ's entry into Jerusalem.

My friendly old barman in the Plaza Mayor reported that Paco had arrived five minutes earlier; was not agitated at my disappearance, and would return in a quarter of an hour, which he did.

Though Paco had arranged for various friends to meet me in the evening, we lunched alone, which I preferred. Having been alone so much of the previous weeks made me a little reluctant to meet four or five strangers all at once – if there had been 20 or so then such a meeting degenerates into a cocktail party atmosphere, and one can concentrate on individuals who seem to be *simpatico* (or ditch them unobtrusively after the regulation five minutes if they are dull) but a party of four or five who are friends of one's host requires more concentration and, in Spain, lasts for many hours. In the meantime Paco and I had much to talk of on such subjects as crossing frontiers illegally, and we imitated Heraclitus, and 'tired the sun with talking and sent him down the sky' – but between times we continued the leisurely sightseeing upon which I had insisted.

I was introduced to the lucky stone frog whose head aspiring undergraduates pat on their way into the Examination Hall and the Colegio de los Irlandeses, founded in 1521 for the training of 30 Irish priests where, alas, they may no longer be found. When I mentioned that books I had read had ascribed the decline in the prosperity of the university to religious bigotry and aristocratic prejudice Paco, as a Catalan (and so an incipient church burner) agreed, but he pointed out – which I had not known – that Queen Isabella's tutor had been a woman, Beatriz de Galinda (1475–1535) at a time when the mere idea of a female don would have shaken all the 'dreaming spires' of Oxford to the point of collapse. Again, in contradiction of the idea that the atmosphere of Salamanca had always been repressive, he told me that when Columbus used to come to Salamanca, to discuss the latest theories of navigation with the self-confessed heretics who followed Copernicus' shocking idea that the earth was not flat, he came as a guest of the Grand Inquisitor himself and, unlike many guests of that dignitary, was free to leave when he chose!

I was shown the Honorary Degree granted to Santa Teresa of Ávila, and the desk at which Fray Luis de Leon had been arrested by the Holy Inquisition, but to which he had returned, after five years in a dungeon, with the enchanting phrase '. . . as I was saying before we were so rudely interrupted'! Next I saw the sixteenth-century stairway leading to the old lecture rooms, adorned with reliefs showing bullfights, and the actual spot where St Juan de Sahagún addressed a charging bull with the words '*Tente necio*' – 'Halt beast' – which brought the infuriated creature to a dead stop in its tracks. (Paco agreed that even if he had done nothing else, this incident alone would have ensured his canonisation in this country!)

Though beginning to feel a little worn by so many varied impressions, I insisted upon visiting my name-saint's Church of St Esteban (locally called Santo Domingo) to see its terrible portrayal of his stoning to death – the future St Paul traditionally among the stoners – and the gentler depiction of his martyrdom by Claudio Coelho. I am continually being surprised by the beauty of this artist's work, hardly known outside Spain, whose fame, I suspect, suffered from the fact that his short life was almost completely spanned by the long one of the incomparable Velasquez.

But out of it all, that which still throbs and glows in my memory is golden, intricately carved exteriors.

First, the Cloisters de las Duenas; then the façade of the Convent of San Esteban and, lastly, the baroque, or plateresque splendours of the gateway to the Universidade Pontificada, with the late sun picking out each perfect, intricate line – escutcheons, medallions and scrolls. There is nothing of its kind to equal these anywhere else in Spain, or in the world. You are at the fountainhead – finer even than Santiago de Compostela itself – though, of course, not 'finer' than Leon (because there never could be competition with another and distant century) but still something so nearly perfect that it can be recalled, together with Leon, without any sense of inadequacy.

I have not forgotten the delightful House of Shells. The shells that are engraved all over its walls are not, apparently, in honour of Santiago, but just a caprice of the architect when he built it, and its delicious, small patio in 1483.

Yet everyone is allowed a private, even modest favourite, and I found myself returning again and again to the Tower of the Clavero.

There is nothing in particular that I can tell you about it beyond the fact that it is a castellated tower with bartizan turrets built in 1480 by Francisco de Sotomayor, the key-warden of the Knightly Order of Alcántara and that, though I had never seen it before, I had dreamed of it countless times.

There is nothing more to say of it save that, in a way, it is beautiful. Perhaps, for me it is a case of that fairly common 'double exposure' memory known, rather vaguely, as 'déjà vu' – but somehow or other, I believe it is a place that has mattered to me intensely at some time I cannot remember.

Paco's party for me in the evening – and that kind of 'evening' in Spain usually means until daylight – was a considerable success from the moment that the other four members realised that they would not have to struggle in their quite good English! I have noticed with myself that I can go through a long session such as this turned out to be in Spanish, though I often express myself in a clumsy way to begin with, and that it leaves me disproportionately tired mentally when it is all over – but this is probably because I am not particularly embarrassed by making mistakes, until I get warmed up, so long as I convey my meaning and capture that of others, nor even by the fact that I speak Spanish with a slight Catalan accent, having learned it when young in Barcelona.

This accent of mine causes a former English friend of mine intense embarrassment on my behalf – though why it should be any worse than a Spanish friend talking English with a slight Scottish accent I cannot, for the life of me, see. It is I, not my listeners, who is doing my hearers the considerable courtesy of relieving them of the need to struggle with my native language. The man who does the favour should not feel apologetic.

After considerable quantities of straw pale 'manzanilla' – first-cousin to the driest sherry you have ever met – we played around with *chanfaina*, *calderillo* and Castile's inevitable, unsurpassable roast suckling pig (of which one really eats only the incredibly crisp, rum-touched 'crackling') and, in due course, an odd cheese called *hornazo*.

The conversation – after the usual, predictable reactions of men in their fifties returning to a place they had known so excitingly in their twenties – drifted towards the occult, after I mentioned, casually, the odd effect the Tower of the Clavero had had on me.

Why, I asked, was there such an almost total ignorance of the subject in Spain? Not ignorance, I was told – or only incidentally so – but total prohibition by the Church, and this prohibition, it emerged, was due to the very reverse of disbelief. Such matters, the Church laid down, were just too dangerous for casual dabbling and, from my own experience, I knew that this was wisdom.

I remembered my acquaintance with Aleister Crowley when I had been in my twenties, and I had seen how obsession with the subject had thrust him remorselessly down the road to madness.

These things, Paco felt, were better handled by the experts. The 'amateur' is quite helpless when faced with the kind of forces that confront him the moment he strays beyond, for example, the silly parlour games of the 'spiritualists' who traded on the desolation of those who had been severed from the beings they most loved by the 1914–18 War, and promised to establish contact for them with the 'Dear Departed'. 'Ghosts' are very rarely indeed the 'souls' or spiritual personalities of those who have died, though often their moods and emotions can be momentarily caught until they die away, like the ripples set up by a fallen stone which, though itself has disappeared, may still be seen and felt for a while. The simpering Old Maids who play around the edge of the bottomless pit, hoping for a cosy 'message' from darling Georgie, are likely unwittingly to release forces of spiritual, or mental destructiveness that neither know nor care of any of their 'Dear Departeds'.

I agreed in general – while in no way discounting the prevalence of occult forces – and added that they are sometimes neither 'good' nor 'evil' in the accepted sense, but simply anarchistic, such as poltergeists, who manifest themselves only where there is a female child just reaching the age of puberty living in, or near the place where the manifestations occur. I mentioned how my reputation had unjustifiably soared overnight when I dealt with such a simple case – which was making the home of some Sinhalese friends intolerable – by the correct use of common salt, and a certain ritual, while I was living in Ceylon. One of Paco's friends said that such a ritual was known, and occasionally used in Spain, and quoted a part of it to me.

However, we agreed that we would give a very wide berth indeed to any of the three gentlemen known to be in possession of the doll-sized, shrunken bodies of unborn children (potentially owners of a soul of great power discovered, like the Dalai Lama, by divination) that play a terrifying rôle in the occult life in that island of magic, white and very black.

But do not imagine that it was a sombre party because we talked, among so many other things, of creatures that move only in the shadow − far from it − though I did occasionally sense the presence of others who, long ago, had trespassed upon this same ground, when to do so would have been to risk the prompt and painful attentions of the Holy Inquisition!

It was pleasant to be in civilised company for a long evening in this ancient place after my long wanderings in the lonely places of Spain − known to the Phoenicians as The Hidden Land − and I spent part of the next day with one or other of the two members of the party who, like Paco, had not yet returned to their homes in other parts of the country, but we confined ourselves to strolling about and doing a little thoughtful drinking. This was because I knew that Paco was determined to take me briefly into the surrounding country before I would be allowed to return to my chosen Road to Compostela, through Leon.

Accordingly, the next day, we set off south into the 5,600 feet highlands of Peña de Francia to pay our respects to the splendid ruined castle of Alba de Tormes, home of the powerful family of Albarez de Toledo, from which the first great Duke of Alba took his title. It was in the Carmelite Convent there that Santa Teresa of Ávila died in 1582.

We played with the idea of following in the footsteps of the Emperor Charles V of the Holy Roman Empire, and first of his name to be King of Spain, who, in 1557, having attempted to dominate the world, then sought to retire from it, all passion spent, in the Monastery of Yuste. There, in the Shangri-La valley known as the Jerandilla de la Vera, facing south from the Gredos Mountains, the exhausted old man of 57 had lived a short year, and exclaimed, 'Here it is Eternal Spring' – and, at last, found rest.

We decided against it, as it was all the time taking me farther away from my ultimate destination, and we settled for a trout lunch at Béjar where, in the Ducal Palace, there is a fascinating sixteenth-century arrangement of fountains, pools, channels and trees known as El Bosque – the Woodland – which is one of the most ingenious examples of landscape gardening that I have seen. Even so, it was late by the time we were back in Salamanca, and we said our farewells (as he was leaving very early for Barcelona) pledging that our next meeting would not be, like this one, after an interval of 35 years!

I had immensely enjoyed Salamanca, with Paco as guide, companion and friend, but now the fun and games were over and my way led due north, through Zamora to Leon.

Zamora was the shorter half of my proposed day's run, lying just over the River Douro which, by now, was beginning to hurry on its way towards the port wine gorges. There I had a pleasant lunch, and was relieved, after my recent – and soon to be repeated – orgy of sightseeing, that it made few demands upon my curiosity. Frontier fortress towns are usually without much interest, and Zamora is no exception.

Zamora – *La Bien Cercada** – was a fortress against the Moors, not the neighbouring Portuguese, and was built as strong as the men of those days could contrive. Its early liberation by Alonso I† of Asturias and Leon in 748 meant that it was one of the earliest major victories of the Reconquest, and in 939 the mighty Emir Abderrahman III left no less than 40,000 of his best warriors in the breaches in the seven walls that he had, at so great a cost, managed to pierce. Almanzor the Terrible (whom we have met earlier) was more successful, capturing and destroying the place in 985, but Ferdinand the Great of Leon and Castile, assisted by El Cid, regained possession and rebuilt it in 1065.

Unfortunately Ferdinand left it in the hands of his daughter

---

* *La Bien Cercada* = The Well Walled, or, more literally, 'well shut in' or 'encircled'.

† Alonsos, as opposed to Alfonsos, occur only among the earliest kings.

Urraca, who refused to hand it over – as according to his will she should have done – to her elder brother, Sancho II. Instead in 1072 it was from her safe stronghold that the regicide Vallido Dolfus was able to slip out to murder Sancho in his camp below by stabbing him in the back, so enabling her to hand over the city to her beloved younger brother Alfonso I of Castile – often, rather confusingly, referred to as Alonso VII of Leon – a very murky page in Spanish history mentioned above when writing of Burgos.

The city came out strongly in favour of 'La Beltraneja' at the time of the death of Henry IV, but surrendered to Ferdinand in 1476, when Isabella had established the illegitimacy of Henry's supposed daughter. The Comuneros held it in 1520 but, after that, history has passed it by.

For a place so early liberated from the Moors its cathedral, built foursquare for defence inside the fortress itself, seems rather a modest affair after the splendours of Salamanca. Belonging to the second half of the twelfth century its nave is only 23 feet wide, and overfilled with a mass of columns. However, it possesses two marvellous canopied tombs. Probably it is most famous for its 1490 choir stalls, beautifully executed, but giving a distinctly Rabelasian impression of contemporary monastic life, with heavy emphasis upon its pederastic aspects. They seem coarse rather than humorous. I have never been accused of prudery, but it seems that twentieth-century pornography is an improvement upon that of the fifteenth!

The so-called Casa del Cid is not convincing. He is known to have lived in Zamora for a while, but there is little real evidence that the battered old building you will see today ever really housed him and his beloved Jimena.

The nature of the country now changes gradually. There is a collection of small lakes as you continue towards Benavente, nourished by the little Rivers Orbigo and Esla, but the once noble Castle of the Pimental family was destroyed by Sir John Moore's troops on their desperate retreat to Coruña. The country of Leon is, appropriately, tawny brown – lion-coloured – and undulating, and notable for little but the endless avenues of poplars following the river banks.

There is a temptation on the run from Zamora to Leon to

turn east to visit Sahagún, where once stood one of the greatest of all the Benedictine abbeys in Spain, if only to say a prayer before the Tomb of King Alonso VI of Asturias and Leon and his matchlessly lovely Moorish-born Queen Zaida, who died in 1109. But although I cannot cure myself of the desire to wander off main roads at the least excuse at least I recognise my weakness, and contented myself with a very much shorter deviation to take a long look at the Castle at Valencia de Don Juan – visually one of the most satisfying of the countless 'once upon a time' castles that make Spain unique. That accomplished I held virtuously on course towards the city which, challenged only by Burgos, is the principal stage along the Pilgrim's Way to Santiago de Compostela, and contains no less than two unequalled tokens of the faith which made the pilgrimage a living reality for a thousand years.

The Roman Septima Gemina Legion chose the site of present-day Leon near the junction of the Rivers Bernesga and Torio, and their descendants continued to hold it against the Gothic horde until as late as the year 586. Though it was swamped by the Moorish onrush of the early eighth century it was, by comparison with most other Moorish-occupied towns, quickly regained by the sword of King Ordoño I in 850. Almanzor – the Scourge of God – again took it in 996, though only after a full year's siege, and burned it to the ground, but by 1002 Ordoño II had achieved its final liberation. Here it was that Ferdinand the Great was crowned not only King of Asturias and Leon, but also of Castile, in 1037, and it quickly became one of the great cities of the Christian Reconquest.

It is easy to become confused in this plethora of kings, but Asturias and Leon got off to an early start. Perhaps some brief explanation may help.

The already Christianised Goths, under King Roderick, suffered a total defeat at the hands of the Moors – who had invaded Spain from what is now called Gibraltar – on the banks of the River Guadalete near the pleasant little sherry town of Jerez de la Frontera in 711. The Christian remnant under the Knight Pelayo were thrown back towards the northern coast, retaining little but a toe-hold in the mountain fastnesses of Asturias, and the caves they sheltered in at Covadonga are one of the places I shall visit on my way home.

There were no less than 30 kings of Asturias and Leon before King Ferdinand added Castile to that title, its rulers hitherto having been only Counts of Castile more or less subservient to the Kings of Asturias and Leon. The kingdoms of Aragón and Navarre survived until the beginning of the fifteenth century when they disappeared in the unity of Spain brought about by the marriage of Ferdinand and Isabella.

Asturias, therefore, always possessed a special position as being the only area of Spain never under Moorish domination – a fact which was recognised even into the present century, when the eldest son and heir of the ruling king or queen of Spain always took the title of Prince of the Asturias, as his counterpart in England does that of Prince of Wales.

The days of Leon's greatness are long over, but it remains unique, first, for its glorious cathedral, where 1,800 metres of superb stained glass fill 125 windows, 57 *oeils-de-boeuf* and wheel-windows and three great rose windows, all this is magically held together by very slender supporting columns, so that the stone work – particularly from inside the building – seems little more than a frame for the glowing bowl of the interior. Some say that Chartres can equal it: I have seen both many times, and award the palm to the *pulchra leonina*.

The building was begun in 1205, and the nave – not in any way exceptional for its size – measures 298 feet by 130, and at its highest point towers to 128 feet. To counteract any feeling of narrowness there are no side chapels – a rarity in Spain – only a kind of crown of them encircling the ambulatory. The largest is dedicated to Santiago, and contains some of the very best of the glass. The whole interior is so spellbinding that it is wiser to see points of the exterior before entering, and this is perhaps best done from the Puerta del Obispo, from whence you can see the extraordinary detail of the apse; the great, but still delicate-seeming flying buttresses, and the plateresque wall of the sacristy.

Once inside you cannot but surrender to the magic wanderings of deepest light upon ancient stone, seen through a hundred transparencies. Shelley's words seem to apply, though he was writing of something else:

> *'Light, like a dome of many coloured glass
> Stains the white radiance of eternity.'*

Everything seems to swim in glowing blues, reds and golds, like the visioned pennants carried by the small devoted band of knights who followed El Cid as he stormed across the sacred soil of Spain. In particular I recommend you to the rose windows in the western and transeptal fronts which, at the hour I was there, were blazing like divine fire.

Once you steady your mind against the bewilderment of ever-shifting colour, then run a finger gently over the smooth grain of the two-tiered choir stalls, the inspired work of Juan de Malines and Diego Copin de Holanda in the fifteenth and sixteenth centuries – the themes they portray escape the bawdiness of those we saw in Zamora. Find your way to Rogier Van der Weyden's 'Pietà', and the mighty sculptured tomb of tenth-century King Ordoño I which serves as the altar, surrounded by the figures of angels, and showing his coat of arms in the keeping of a herald and a friar.

There is a touch of the strictly mundane in the great Tomb of the Condesa Sancha upon which her nephew, heir and murderer is portrayed, suffering his just deserts by being torn to pieces by wild horses – but she *was* very rich, and no doubt seemed to him to be bent upon donating all his inheritance to the cathedral before he had had a chance to enjoy it!

For the rest you must just wander – but be careful, as here you are surrounded by much still potent magic, including the image of the Virgin which bleeds whenever an unrepentant gambler enters her chapel. Here, too, anyone perjuring an oath will surely die within the year. This is the eternal Spain which neither H-bombs nor package tours have the power to destroy.

As though the possession of one of the most beautiful cathedrals in Christendom – perhaps the most beautiful – were not enough for this town of only about 100,000 inhabitants, there is at least one other building here in Leon to make the place unique.

This is the Basilica of San Isidro,* whose body was brought

---

* St Isidro the Doctor, not his lazy namesake of Madrid who slept while the angels laboured on his behalf. c.s.

from Seville. At its consecration in 1063 by Ferdinand the Great there were no less than five saints-to-be present, and it is one of the few places in the Catholic world where a Host may be visible at all times – another, strangely enough, being in nearby Lugo.

Built on the site of a church of St John the Baptist, it was the pantheon of all the early kings of Asturias, Leon and Castile until desecrated by the troops of Napoleon's Marshal Soult, ghoulishly searching for trinkets. As I said above, I deplore the tendency to liken one thing with another, but I am unable to resist the saying that St Isidro is the Sistine Chapel of the Romanesque.

The low ceilings and every inch of wall space is active with simulated life – and death. Tales from the Gospels, scenes of contemporary life, the men and women in their distinctive native dress, others brawling outside a tavern, still more picking grapes from the taller vines of 900 years ago, killing the Martinmas pig, boxing matches: all side by side with many marvels and miracles of the spirit; strange monsters slithering through exotic flora – the mind reels at so much vivid movement. Then, suddenly, in the groined vault of the Saint's tomb there are our old friends the signs of the zodiac (of 'What the Stars Foretell' fame) and an apocalyptic vision of St John, one hand holding the curved double-edged sword and the other the Book sealed with the Seven Secret Seals, and, behind him, the Seven Churches of Asia, the ruins of some of which I visited, myself not long ago in present-day Turkey.

However, the central composition of the pantheon is a superb, Dantesque Last Supper and, in the background, the shepherds, listening to the news of Christ's birth while herds of goats playfully butt one another, and a big sheepdog laps from a stream. It is truly one of the most extraordinary buildings that I have ever seen anywhere – and I did not need to be reminded that on the night before the critical Battle of Tolosa in 1212 there was heard the sound of a mighty mailed fist beating upon the heavy wooden door, and a great voice crying, 'It is El Cid who calls Saint Isidro to the aid of Christ in Spain tomorrow on the field of Las Navas de Tolosa!'

This was the battle which was the beginning of the end of

Moorish power in the country – from that day on they were always, except locally and temporarily, on the defensive.

Leon's third marvel, though a lesser one, had changed its character since last I had been there. What had been the Convent of San Marcos, founded by the Knights of Santiago, who devoted their lives to keeping the Road safe for the pilgrims, was built in 1168, but entirely rebuilt early in the sixteenth century, with a sumptuous plateresque façade. Then it had been reduced to the ignominy of a barracks (after the fashion of the Portuguese with far too many of their historic buildings), though the entrance was always dominated by the now familiar figure of 'Santiago Matamoros'.

Today it has been taken over by the State Tourist Department, and run as a five-star parador. Paco having refused to let me pay for most of my stay in Salamanca, I felt that I could justifiably revel in its splendours for a couple of nights. I wanted another full day in Leon to obtain permission to view an illuminated Bible, dated 960, and I wanted to see the place where in 1065 Ferdinand the Great – attacked by what he knew to be a fatal fever – had chosen to pass his last hours before the Shrine of San Isidro, and perhaps to take just one more wander in the coloured darkness of the cathedral before I continued towards the west.

Let me say at once that, while the original idea of my old friend Luis Bolin to save some of Spain's crumbling heritage by turning places of beauty into superb hotels was wholly right at the time he undertook it – a time when Spain had few tourists and very little foreign exchange to house them adequately if they came – I now occasionally feel that, since his death, the idea is in danger of being carried too far. The architects concerned – previously sadly cramped for the means to carry out his plans – are now being given financial *carte blanche*, and so are overdoing it. The parador at Leon is such a case – what was intended to be sombrely splendid comes near to being vulgarly ostentatious – but, so far, there have been few serious lapses.

The old Hostel of San Marcos was, like Leon itself, of particular importance to the Pilgrims, since they arrived here not only by the conventional route from the east, and from Valládolid and the south, but also from overseas to Oviedo – or more precisely, from one or other of the Asturian capital's various small Biscayan ports, and then fought their way up from there through the incredible 4,000 feet pass of Pajares.

My second day did not hang heavily on my hands as, in addition to what I had planned, I found the house of the man who discovered Florida – Juan Ponce de Leon – sat a while beside the great baroque fountain of Neptune in the Public Gardens of San Francisco, and finally fell in love with the thousand-years-old Mozarabic Church of San Miguel de Escalada, with its horseshoe-shaped arches that are such an unmistakable sign of the Moorish presence.

Leon, unlike Salamanca, does not flaunt its treasures – apart from the Cathedral and San Isidro – but, like Segovia, unveils them one by one to the patient or observant wanderer. Clearly I must go back there sometime yet once again and get myself comprehensively lost in the almost unnoticed Old Town. I now realised that, even after half a dozen visits, and its relatively small size, I still have much more to discover in Leon.

8. The Pilgrim's Way – Leon to Santiago de Compostela

The pilgrims must have left Leon physically and spiritually refreshed, but sharply conscious that they were entering upon one of the hardest and most dangerous stages of their long road.

Although they could leave the savage Cantabrican Range – rising to over 8,000 feet – to the north, they still had to break through the substantial barrier of the Mountains of Leon, called El Bierzo, between them and Compostela, including the highest point of the entire pilgrimage.

The first one or two days' march to Astorga was easy going, and there were no problems – at least in general – in crossing the River Obrigo by the bridge which still stands, and claims to be one of the oldest in Spain. I say 'in general' as it was precisely here that a certain Don Suero de Quiñones, having been rejected by his lady-love, elected to make a nuisance of himself on 11 July 1434, when he denied passage to all knights until they had first jousted with him.

In the best Arthurian tradition challengers turned up in droves, and were duly pitched into the Obrigo by the redoubtable (if slightly potty) Don Suero. Each evening he gave a banquet to those whom he had overthrown during the previous day, defeating no less than 727 challengers in the space of 30 days. As by this time the exercise had enabled him to overcome his passion for his reluctant girlfriend, he graciously al-

21 *Part of the highly intricate carvings around the Portico de la Gloria of the Cathedral of Santiago*

22 *One of the more open and friendly valleys in the grim Montes de Leon*

lowed traffic – including pilgrims – to continue on their way! He lived for another 24 years, when he was killed by one of the knights he had defeated while holding the bridge over the Obrigo.

As an aside, there is a Spanish literary belief that Don Suero was Cervantes' model for Don Quixote. More or less supporting this theory is the fact that Cervantes' aunt married a man called Alfonso Quejada, a direct descendant of the knight who ultimately killed Don Suero – but it is all little more than another 'Who really wrote Shakespeare's plays?' kind of controversy, which enjoys an occasional airing in literary clubs and societies when they cannot think of anything more promising for discussion.

Assuming that Don Suero was not around at the time, even the less sturdy pilgrims expected to reach Astorga from Leon in two days, and the hearty ones did the whole 30 miles in a single, normal day, and, once there, they could be sure of food, shelter and protection again. In fact, by the eleventh century, the Astorga which Pliny described as 'a magnificent city' had crumbled away under the buffetings of Almanzor and the Reconquest, to which could be added the fact that it had the misfortune to become a favourite bone of contention between the Kings of Leon and the Counts of Castile.

So complete was its destruction that it had had to be more or less rebuilt from its own ruins in the twelfth century, precisely for the protection of pilgrims, though you can still see part of its original Roman walls, 20 feet thick even though stripped of their facings. Though it thus served a useful purpose during the great centuries of Faith, it again suffered almost total destruction at the hands of Napoleon's Marshal Junot. So, with the combined efforts of Messrs Almanzor and Junot, ably abetted by numerous Kings of Leon and Counts of Castile, it is hardly surprising that today it is a sad-looking little town of less than 10,000 inhabitants, though the cathedral is magnificent.

From it Mount Teleno looms surprisingly near, and the big peaks to the north stand out menacingly. For those who walked all this way in their millions, an added sense of alarm must have been the presence of the Maragatos who, I am glad to say, are still in this area today, and largely unchanged in

23   *The Cathedral of Santiago de Compostela*

looks, clothes or beliefs, though there has been a slight tendency for them to retreat to the remoter valleys and villages of that spur of the Mountains of Leon known as El Bierzo.

The Maragatos are descendants of Berber highlanders, who came with the Moorish invasion of the early eighth century. They have kept their blood remarkably pure – marriage with a Spaniard being heavily discouraged by their elders – startlingly handsome, fierce and, though technically Christian, observing all the tribal customs they brought with them from Northern Africa 1300 years ago, some of them very strange.

Thus, a proposal of marriage is made by a suitor laying straw along the way that leads from her house to his. If the girl – duly chaperoned at this stage – does not follow the route marked out for her in this way before sunset of the following day, then the suitor knows that he has been rejected. The men wear zouave-like breeches, and the women much jewellery – in fact their entire dowry – fashioned in strange, antique designs that I have seen nowhere else, not even in those parts of Africa from which they originally came.

At one time the Maragatos handled most of the inter-village carrier trade of northern Spain (which included correspondence among the few literate ones of their world and, more particularly, between different monasteries and convents) and you will still occasionally see a caravan of them leading strings of magnificent mules – far superior to the scruffy Spanish variety – peddling their wares, and particularly their unique jewellery, among the mountain valleys of Leon and Asturias.

Their dances, if you are lucky enough to come across them (and no package tour guide could 'fix' one for you, as with some gipsy 'flamenco' group in Granada), are danced with the measured dignity of an ancient ritual, wholly un-Spanish.

After Astorga comes the long, slogging climb over the Manzanal Pass, often snow-blocked in January and February, and there are few signs of wayside help until you reach the converted synagogue, and the strong castle of the Dukes of Frias at Bembibre, leading down to the River Sil and the once strong town of Ponferrada.

As with Astorga, Ponferrada – originally the Roman 'Interamnium Flavium' – had to be rebuilt from its own ruins, so often had the tides of war passed over it, and it was only in the thirteenth century that the Knights Templar built the castle which still dominates the place. It looks its age, with tall flowering grasses growing between the mighty blocks of uneven stone of which it is composed, but still proud with coronetted turrets in best fairy-tale tradition, imposing, but visibly nearing the end of the cycle that will return it to the earth from whence it came.

But even Ponferrada was only a breathing space before setting off upon the hardest and highest stage of the whole Pilgrims' Way. The main mass of the mountains of Leon was behind, but a wicked spur of them known as El Bierzo still barred the road to the softer, easier lands of Galicia and their great objective of Santiago itself.

To begin with it is pleasant enough, running through Tyrolean-like scenery, alive with the sounds of birdsong and running water, and bright with wild flowers, immensely tall, slim poplars and apple orchards – for we are near the great cider-producing land of Asturias. But each side valley seems to be dotted with literally hundreds of tiny, mushroom-like hermitages, chapels and sanctuaries, some a full thousand years old, – this apart from the tenth-century Mozarabic church of Santo Tomas de las Ollas. Many of them were created under the influence and encouragement of Saint Fructuoso, as refuges from the first great wave of Moorish invasion – half churches, half anchorite cells, designed solely to keep the Faith alive – and you will discover a score or more, unmentioned by even the most painstaking of guide books, in any number of remote valleys, seemingly forgotten as they crouch among the thick bracken.

But, by the time you reach Villafranca del Bierzo, you will be glad of the sun of Spain, for it is a desolate place in rough weather. For the pilgrims Villafranca was 'a city of comfort', though for many it signified the end of their great endeavour. The embattled, round red church of Santiago in Villafranca had special powers to grant all those that had fallen sick the same Indulgences that they had hoped to receive at the Tomb of the Apostle. If they had got as far as this, Mother Church obviously felt, then the sincerity of their intentions to get there had been amply proven, and they could rest peacefully, waiting either for death or for the day when they were strong enough to begin the long journey home.

Today there are still some 5,000 people who gather round the sixteenth-century fortified palace of the Dukes of Alba, and there is a Government-operated 'albergue' to cater for modern transients such as myself. From there you could arrange to visit any of the surrounding circles of once great monasteries, by mule or donkey, such as that of Carracedolo, founded in 990 and rebuilt in 1138 – though you will need to be equipped both with a taste for complete solitude and plenty of warm clothes! Once you stray off the track beaten by the feet of the pilgrims you are, in every sense, off the beaten track, and this I have felt more strongly in El Bierzo than in many factually far more remote places.

Before leaving the subject of this strange, rather hostile-feeling little town, I should, perhaps, mention that it contains a collegiate church rebuilt in 1726, and a large Franciscan Convent founded in 1550 by Pedro de Toledo, once Spanish Viceroy of Naples.

For those pilgrims who had the strength to resist the temptation of receiving substitute Indulgences at the church of Santiago, there now came the still more testing stretch through the Pass of Piedrafita – in fact only a score or so feet higher than that of Manzanal between Astorga and Ponferrada, but possessing a desolate kind of magnificence before which the heart readily quails. There is a stone cross there, 3,638 feet above sea level, and from beside it a tremendous view to peaks more than twice as high again.

Here we brush against history again, as at this point it was decided to hurl into a ravine the last 150,000 golden guineas of Sir John Moore's Army Chest to prevent it falling into French hands. This was in January 1809, and despite having drunk all the wine they could find in Ponferrada, hundreds of Englishmen died here of the bitter cold, but Paget's rearguard turned and fought off the pursuing French cavalry, and the tattered remnants of the doomed force staggered on to Coruña.

Today's main road drops slowly to Lugo, but most of the pilgrims turned gratefully southwestwards towards Sarria and the sheltered valley of the River Miño. Immediately you feel that you are out of the harsh kingdom of Leon, and in the gentler, damper province of Galicia.

On this occasion I headed for Lugo for the night, with the intention of taking a swing from there through the little-known country towards Orense, one of the very few Spanish cities which I had never seen, even *en passant*.

Lugo is justly proud of its 30–40 feet high slate Roman walls, 20 feet thick and with no less than 85 circular defensive bastions. It possesses a cathedral, but it has been somewhat downgraded: whereas once it had been the see of an archbishop it now supports only a suffragan bishop dependent upon Santiago de Compostela – not quite cashiered, but certainly reduced to the ranks! Part of it dates from 1129, but the mixture of different architectural periods – usually so successfully achieved in Spain – is uninspired and rather confusing, and I felt that I had seen all the cathedrals I wanted for a while in Leon, and so, instead of improving my mind, wasted a couple of daylight hours in watching various very amateur fishermen, not far from the Santiago gate, collecting what seemed to me an amazingly large number of salmon, trout and lampreys from the waters of the River Miño. I could, more informatively perhaps, have sought out the five – no less – pilgrim hostels Lugo once supported.

I knew, of course, that there was superlative fishing to be had in Galicia and, even more so, in the mountains of Asturias, and had planned to take a look at it on my return journey, but this miraculous draught of fishes so near to a fairly large town was a surprise. I suppose that since there is little industrialisation in this part of Spain the rivers are unpolluted to a degree that is today rare in Britain.

Alas, the sense of change on leaving the austere heights of Leon for the sheltered, often misty lowlands of Galicia is not caused only by the change of climate, but also by distressing fact that people now seemed to me to be talking in Portuguese rather than in *castillano* and, while the latter is one of the noblest of all spoken tongues, the former is little more than a gobbling, sibilant dialect. In Galicia itself this humble status as a dialect called *gallego* is accepted, but the Portuguese have the

nerve to claim that it is something more than a sorry mis-
pronunciation of Spanish!

Fairly early for me, due to a night haunted by train-
shuntings, I was on my way south, on a road which did not
appear to have received much in the way of repairs since pilgrim days, through Sarria to Monforte de Lemos. Once there, I
knew that this was to be one of my lucky days as I ran more or
less straight into a wedding celebration, to which the 'music'
was being supplied by a pair of the famous blind bagpipers of
Galicia of which I had been told, but had never previously seen
– or, more precisely, heard. Was this Gala Night in Galashiels
or a wedding in remotest Galicia?

My polite, and obviously sincere interest was swiftly rewarded by an invitation to a place beside the bridegroom's
father – a chirpy little cricket of a man who had obviously
already sampled the various large earthenware jugs of pale red
wine. There I was able to watch and listen to renderings of the
Danza Prima of Astorga and the *Muineira* – the Miller's Wife –
of Galicia. Though gay enough, they were much quieter than
the ferocious Aragonese *jotas* that I had witnessed a few weeks
before near the Pyrenees.

These highly skilled bagpipers are peculiar to this part of
Spain, though how a kind of cult for them to be blind arose I
have never discovered, but friezes in churches along the latter
stages of the road to Santiago depict them as they were 700
years or so ago, and as they still are today.

I was inevitably obliged to eat a large number of sweet
bizcochos – a special kind of biscuit as light on the stomach as
a pound of lead and, within an hour, I had made my hosts a
total gift of my capacity for digestion for the next day or so.
Having succeeded, however, in making nothing but the politest
sounds of gratitude in departure which, alas, are not the same
here as they are in the Arab world (where only the loudest of
belches is acceptable tribute to the generosity of one's host) I
stole away to the skirl of the pipes towards the castle-crowned
hill and the sixteenth-century church of San Vicente del Pino.

There I fell in with a retired priest, 85 years old, but with a
kindly twinkle in his old eye, who offered to take me to the
seventeenth-century baroque Jesuit Institute, which was the

prime reason for my visit to Monforte de Lemos. On the way I was compelled to listen to his rhapsodies upon the wonders of Leeds where, it emerged, Father Manuel had once, long ago, spent a single night, which provided him with his most treasured memory though, I am sorry to say, of a nature far removed from his later, celibate, calling.

With only a little difficulty I found not only five El Grecos – three of them in perfect condition and quite unmistakably genuine – but also four magnificent canvases by the sixteenth-century artist Andrea del Sarto.

A small boy of twelve or so was briskly dusting them off with a feather brush of the type usually associated with purely domestic activities but, knowing my Spaniards, I did not express alarm at his cavalier handling of his priceless charge, only surprise that one so young should know so well how to look after such valuable property. I do not think that he had previously considered that they might be particularly valuable, but he immediately began to treat them as though they were, and told me that they were supposed to have been painted in Toledo by a Greek gentleman at the orders of the King – that meant way back before the Civil War!

Dare I hope that my tact has prolonged the life of a tremendous treasure trove? However, I could not help wondering why collectors throughout the world did not stop fighting one another at the art sales of the world with, literally, hundreds of thousands of pounds in the hope of possessing just one of such canvases as were now before me, when they could no doubt acquire one or two tactfully for a few hundred in the remoter corners of Spain! Perhaps such methods would be illegal – but I have known art dealers who occasionally bent the law here and there, particularly transcontinental ones. Alternatively, why does not the Spanish Ministerio de Bellas Artes – Ministry of Fine Arts – carry them off to the Prado in Madrid so that the whole world can see them?

I told Father Manuel that, after passing through Orense, I might have time to find my way to the Cistercian Monastery of Santa Maria la Real de Osera and, perhaps, San Lorenzo de Carboeira near Lalin.

His cheerful old face immediately became anxious, although

he had nothing against the two places I had mentioned, but he told me that I must be very careful to avoid the several 'black' churches in the area, which contained blasphemous paintings of gryphons drinking from the chalice that contained the Blood of Christ, while a Lion of Judah, with a witch-cat, or 'familiar', looked on. The monks, he assured me, had even been accused of recommending pilgrims to fraudulent Inns in Compostela where they were fleeced and, if rich, occasionally murdered for their possessions. Certain, it seemed, that at some time in the Middle Ages, the inmates of some of the 'religious' houses in that area had practised Black Rites, and were tried and excommunicated – or had something similar happened relatively recently, and tales of it lingered on in the age-muddled memory of Father Manuel?

I felt attracted to the idea of attempting a kind of reconstruction of the crime on the spot, but in such cases informative sources are almost always carefully destroyed or, at best, removed to the Church's most secret archives. I noted it only, therefore, as a small, dark mystery I might try to unravel if time and circumstances should one day allow it.

It was with regret that I bade farewell to my new friends and the El Grecos. How delightful it would have been to pop the latter into the back of the car with me; how much richer would I have thereby made the world's readily available artistic heritage and, incidentally, how much richer I should myself have become in the process!

Orense, like Lugo, stands on the now familiar River Miño, soon to become the Portuguese frontier River Minho. At Orense it is spanned by a notable bridge – so notable that one might reasonably wonder whether it did not include an element of superfluous effort in that it stands no less than 135 feet above the normal level of the river. However, the 150 feet long central span is an impressive example of thirteenth- and fifteenth-century engineering, replacing a still earlier structure. Here John of Gaunt made his 'capital' during his brief 'reign' in 1386–7.

The cathedral, dedicated to St Martin, was founded as long ago as the year 572, but what you see today is partly twelfth and partly thirteenth century. The portal beneath the narthex, known as 'El Paraiso' is an indifferent copy of the Portica de la Gloria of Santiago de Compostela, remarkable chiefly for the fact that you can still clearly see that much of its ornamentation was originally painted in bright colours.

Driving due west, through the undemandingly pleasing countryside, often reminiscent of Southern Ireland rather than of Spain, I passed leisurely through Ribadavia, with its ruined Dominican monastery-residence of the self-styled 'Kings' of Galicia of the tenth century. I noticed the peculiar granite pillars, used since time immemorial to support the vines that produce the over-sweet local red wine – as mentioned much earlier, mediaeval vines were not cropped down to the short, compact bushes, almost universal in modern vineyards – and continued through La Cañiza to Puenteareas, when I felt that I had earned a drink and a short rest while considering where I should spend the coming night.

Vigo was an obvious possibility, but Vigo is a bustling, rather noisy port and – more menacing still – right on the track of potential package tours. The last time I had been there I had gone aboard a liner to pay my respects to the late and very great Pablo Casals (I had met him several times during the Civil War) who, in his eighties was on his honeymoon with his beautiful 20-odd years old South American wife. Someone had asked him if he had played at all during the crossing, and he had replied, 'No. But I kept up my finger work every day.'

I decided for a place without memories, and headed on to spend a delightfully peaceful night at the parador at Tuy, with the fertile Vale of the River Louro behind me, and the winding Miño-Minho far below.

Tuy is unexpected. It stands on a cliff above the river, almost opposite the Portuguese fortress of Valença do Minho, whose garrison had successfully defeated Marshal Soult's attempt to cross in 1809, after the defeat of Sir John Moore. Since the river constitutes the frontier do not indulge in a capricious midnight swim as, if you do so, both sides will, pardonably, assume that you are a smuggler – though, in fact, I should think what little smuggling goes on there today is by mutual agreement!

Tuy was chosen as his 'capital' by the Gothic king Witizo in about A.D. 698, but Ferdinand II chose the present site in 1170. It has a fortress-like cathedral, part of it dating from the thirteenth century – notably the west portal – but most of what stands so stolidly today belongs to the fifteenth and sixteenth centuries. It is dedicated to San Telmo, patron of Spanish sailors, who is the same gentleman renowned elsewhere as St Elmo, whose fireballs clinging to the yards of a ship were always regarded as a favourable omen though, may I add, the only time I saw them on a thousand-ton ship off the west coast of Africa, I was far more scared than I cared to admit.

The kneeling figure in San Telmo's large chapel dates from 1579 and is of Bishop Diego de Torquemada, of the same family as the founder of the Holy Inquisition a century earlier, and here, too, is the grave of Bishop Lucas de Tuy, who spent most of his time persecuting followers of the Albigensian heresy – perhaps not quite the right place for a visiting Orangeman!

You will notice at once the great metal braces binding together the whole structure of the cathedral. These date from Lisbon's great earthquake on All Souls Day of 1755, when the whole of western and southern Spain, though so far from its epicentre, rocked and swayed like a ship in a storm. Tuy seems to lie along one of those seams in the earth's crust which are earthquake prone, as it had other severe shakings in the sixteenth century of which Portugal was not the origin.

Running north next day I had my first sight of the sea for what seemed to me to have been a long time when, bypassing Vigo, I headed for Pontevedra. Here I found arcaded streets, stone-built but lined inside with dark wood, necessary against the prevalent 'Scotch' mist of this part of Spain for eight out of the twelve months of the year, and some fine old granite houses bearing armorial shields. There are various other buildings that give the place a pleasant air of antiquity, from the baroque San Bartolomé to the ruins of the fourteenth-century Convent of Santo Domingo, but I paused only to take a more detailed look at the conspicuous, round Pilgrim's Chapel, built in the eighteenth century, which seemed rather modern by pilgrimage standards.

For a while now we shall be in the land of the 'rias', which have been variously described as 'fjords' and 'firths'. I prefer to call them 'rias', as they are infinitely less precipitous than the few fjords I once saw in Norway, and noticeably less bleak than the many firths I have seen in Scotland. You will see what I mean if you now turn aside to one of the most beautiful of all Galicia's rias – that of Arosa.

The few tourists you will meet will be mostly from Vigo, though you may encounter some solemn Danes 'enjoying' the radioactive saline springs of La Toja, but it is a beautiful stretch of water, with undemanding little seaside resorts, excellent deep-sea fishing, water-skiing and sailing, with small ferry-boats bobbing and weaving between the islands of Arosa, Salvora and Ons, among others. Somehow it put me in mind of my school-boy holidays at my grandfather's old house near Seaview in the Isle of Wight in the 1920s – and this is intended as a compli-ment, and not cynically. Villagarcia de Arosa and Cambados are the 'capitals' of the area – pleasant, bright old fishing vil-lages, noisy with gulls, where 'old salts' will take you out in their slightly decrepit row-boats after mackerel or whiting, just as their opposite numbers did for me in England forty years ago. I recommend the still unspoiled sandy bathing beaches of Ayros below Sangenjo if the sun is shining.

On our way we pass many of the unmistakable stone barns built on stilts, peculiar to Galicia, each bearing a stone cross at either end. They look like some kind of open-air tomb, but they are built in this way against the prevailing damp westerly winds from the Atlantic, and only incidentally to thwart ver-min, both winged and four footed, and contain nothing more sinister than farm produce, and the instruments connected with the cultivation of some neighbouring plot of the rich soil.

But although the Ria de Arosa may be a pleasant, unspoiled holiday setting, particularly attractive for children who tend to wilt, rather than benefit in the oven heat of a Mediterranean July or August, I am heading back towards my objective, which now is near. Only a few miles from the head of the ria, on the little River Ulla, lies the unpretentious town of Padrón, where St James the Apostle, or Santiago, first landed on Spanish soil, and the place to which his miraculous ship re-turned with his body after his martyrdom for burial in Com-postela, as was related earlier. From here came the scallop shells with which the pilgrimage is so closely associated – though those who could afford it bought one from the silversmiths who flourished from the trade once the pilgrimage was established.

The thirteenth-century bridge over the Ulla was built on foundations laid by the Romans, who called the place Iria Flavia. It is in no sense treated as a holy place, though no less than 28 bishops chose to be buried in its collegiate church, and the road climbs the Sar Valley, passing the baroque pilgrimage church where once criminals could find sure sanctuary.

If we were true pilgrims we should not be approaching Santiago from the south, but from the east, through Mellid, and then climbing the hill which they named Mountjoy, as from it they caught their first glimpse of the three bell towers of the great cathedral. It must have been a moment of very real joy for most of them, after all the dangers and hardships that they had suffered, a kind of joy for which there is no real present-day equivalent.

I think that to attempt a full description of the cathedral would inevitably fail – all that I have read of it at least partly fails – so I will try to confine myself largely to facts, and leave the overwhelmingly strong atmosphere of the place to reach you by photographs or, far better, by a personal pilgrimage, as the place is, and must always be, an intensely personal experience.

For 800 years or so it has ranked after only Jerusalem and Rome as a place of spiritual fulfilment, and the Portico de la Gloria, was, quite literally, the 'Portus Quietus' of millions. Here they could unburden themselves of all the failures of the past and, if God so willed it, begin a new life, of which the colours were, once again, bright with hope.

At the Portico de la Gloria Christ is portrayed in all his glory, showing his wounds, surrounded by saints and angels. At his feet is Saint James, leaning on his pilgrim's staff, but seated on a throne set on the back of lions, though his bare feet rest upon green grass. This is a very benign St James, far removed from Santiago Matamoros of Logroño and many other places. Behind the principal figures are the Evangelists and the four and twenty Elders of the Apocalypse with their musical instruments. It cannot be adequately described in words, perhaps the nearest approach being made in my hearing when, after gazing at it for a few minutes, my companion said, 'This is not sculpture; this is frozen music.'

The figure of the artist who created all this, known to us only as Master Mathew, kneels before his God – or, before this, his masterpiece to the Glory of God.

You will certainly not overlook the great Tree of Jesse, between the lower stems of which pilgrims placed their spread hands in respect and prayer – and still do so – while saying the obligatory five Hail Marys, or while begging for some great favour. So many millions of supplications have left five hollows worn in the iron-hard stone,* so for us to add our own will do no harm.

The gold and jewelled figure of the Apostle dominates the High Altar – indeed, by its placement, it draws your eyes wherever you may be in the huge 310 feet long building – and this particular figure is always illuminated, day and night, even on the Friday and Saturday of Easter Week when, in Catholic churches, all lights are put out until there comes the great Sunday morning cry of 'Christ is Risen'. The illumination is provided by a silver lamp presented by Gonsalvo de Cordoba – the man who epitomises the final achievement of the Reconquest. El Cid represents rather the dedicated resolution to fight for that end, not for its achievement.

There are two crypts, but the silver urn containing the remains of the Apostle and his two disciples Sts Theodore and Athanasius is in that below the Capilla Mayor, and you descend a few shallow, narrow steps in order to see it. Whatever your particular creed may be, centuries of devotion have made this a very holy place.

Far earlier I related the Golden Legend of how the Apostle's martyred body arrived by sea at Padrón and, after many diffi-

---

* This put me in mind of Justinian's pillar in San Sofia in Istanbul. It is related that the Emperor, while kneeling in prayer there, suddenly experienced a terrible headache which, when he leaned his forehead against the pillar, instantly disappeared. Since then the millions who, in trouble or distress, have placed a finger against the same spot, have worn a hole three inches deep into the porphyry. c.s.

culties, was finally buried here, and also of how his where-abouts were revealed early in the ninth century by the *campus stellae* – the starry field – that gave Compostela its name. Then came the small chapel built by Alonso II and enlarged by Alonso III, Kings of Asturias in the ninth and tenth centuries, which was totally destroyed by Almanzor who, though he en-slaved the population to drag the church's bells across half Spain to adorn his tremendous mosque in Córdoba, still left the Apostle's tomb inviolate.*

The Apostle's determination not to be moved was strongly revealed at a much later date, when 'the pirate Drake' (as Philip II impolitely called him) landed at Coruña, and the Archbishop began to open the tomb to take the sacred relics elsewhere to safety when, as many witnesses confirmed, 'there was a mighty wind, and a great light from the tomb, so that he was forced to desist'.

The 'new' cathedral, as it stands today, was built between 1100 and 1130, and actually incorporates the Saint's tomb into its structure and, from being at first purely a local place of pilgrimage, became universal. Chaucer's Wife of Bath had been in 'Galice at Seynt Jame', and John of Gaunt chose to be crowned here in 1386, when he made his unsuccessful bid to claim the throne of Castile on behalf of his wife, daughter of Pedro the Cruel. Napoleon's Marshal Ney appropriated the contents of the Treasury in 1809 and, although he found it disappointing, left the Apostle in peace – the poverty of the treasury being hardly surprising since, due to the Reformation, the number of pilgrims had dwindled from half a million to a few thousand a year by Ney's time but, strangely enough, to-day the figure is again rising steadily.

The original early twelfth-century interior has been encased with both baroque and plateresque portals which in themselves are works of art of the very highest order, rich in detail and pictorial fascination. That known as the Obradorio is basically Romanesque, and fronts on to the main Cathedral Square, and you must circle the great mass of the building if you wish to

* This is more credible than it might appear at first sight, as educated Moslems have a great reverence for Jesus and St John the Baptist as Holy Men. They merely deny the former's Divinity. c.s.

see that of Las Platerias (the Silversmiths), La Quintana and the Azabacheria. These depend a great deal for full appreciation upon the time of day, and so on the intensity and angle of light at different hours – this applies particularly to the Obradorio, many of its incredible intricacies being lost if seen in shadow.

But it is the astonishingly rich interior that will draw you back again and again, for it seems as though, by some magical chance, everything in it is the finest of its age. The finest Romanesque, baroque and plateresque; the finest tapestries of Goya, Bayeu, Teniers and Rubens; custodias by the unique master of his art, Enrique de Arfe, who came to Spain from Flanders with Philip the Fair in 1505; gold and precious stones; the finest wrought-iron grilles, so that after a while the figures of Apostles and Old Testament characters take on an almost personal reality in the silent, semi-darkness of the great building.

When Santiago's Day of 25 July falls on a Sunday – as in 1976 – it becomes a Jubilee Year, and an otherwise sealed door into the cathedral – the 'Puerta Santa' – is ceremonially opened for pilgrims. Also, on that day, and certain others, you will see the world-famous *botafumeiro* in use. It consists of a gigantic silver censer suspended by a chain from the highest point of the principal nave. It is normally only on show in the Treasury, but on High Days and Holydays it is brought in by seven men, filled with incense and set alight. This done, the botafumeiro is lifted clear of the floor by ropes and pushed, apparently quite gently, to and fro, gradually gaining a rhythmic momentum. Flames and clouds of aromatic smoke, against the background of the soaring music of the great organ and massed choirs continues 'crescendo', until the gigantic censer almost touches the immensely remote roof of the basilica like a flaming meteor then, surprisingly quickly, with the accompanying music growing steadily fainter, it is slowed to a standstill, and removed by the seven stalwarts.

This dates from the times when the first pilgrims bivouacked inside the cathedral, often for days before the Feast of the Apostle, and was done 'to purify the air' – no doubt very necessary, bearing in mind the season of the year in which the Apostle's Day is celebrated, and the ideas – or lack of them – concerning crowd hygiene prevalent in the Middle Ages with, always looming, the inevitable danger of the plague.

Practical as always, it was just this aspect of the Great Pilgrimage that led Ferdinand and Isabella to press forward with the building of the huge pilgrims' hostelry known as the Hospital Real in the opening years of the sixteenth century. As in Leon, one of the city's greatest buildings has now been turned into a luxury hotel, and even if you cannot afford it for long – as I most certainly cannot – try to manage it for a single night. Prices, of course, vary enormously according to season in this part of Spain, and the nearer your visit is to 25 July the more expensive it will become.

The main façade of the Hospital Real – now the Hostal de los Reyes Catolicos – was built as late as 1766–72, and stands directly beside the cathedral's 'Fachada del Obradorió', which is reached from the plaza by graceful, quadruple flights of steps, and flanked in the background by the two great 230 feet high towers, so you are always conscious of your nearness to the great heart of the pilgrimage, despite the comforts that surround you.

You enter the Hostal through a superb plateresque portal, and actually within the building are two exquisite Renaissance patios, two courtyards and a chapel which dates from 1556. Then again there is the Sala Real, with murals by Arias Varela, including portraits of Ferdinand and Isabella, and another of Charles IV (a depressing subject) by Goya, painted in his most vitriolic vein. However, do not let this seem too overwhelming as a place wherein to rest a night. The internal modernisation rarely loses sight of the fact that visitors are there to seek rest after sightseeing rather than in search of still more, and its task is to give you the service and comfort expected from a five star hotel.

To descend from the sublime to what, if not the ridiculous, is at least the strictly mundane, the Hostal has two dining rooms and a seafood bar-restaurant (where I spent a long gourmet's evening), not to mention such things as a nightclub, various bars *and* a bowling alley!

One of the first things that you will notice about Santiago de Compostela, once you have absorbed the strongly contrasting emotions promoted by the cathedral and the Hostal de los

24 *Santiago de Compostela, the roof looking like a gigantic set of chessmen*

Reyes Catolicos, is that there is a very great deal more to see, and that its narrow, arcaded streets lead to a university founded in 1532. In its library, you may view the richly illuminated Book of Hours that belonged to Ferdinand the Great in 1055.

Perhaps even more rapidly you will notice, either with pleasure or regret, the Englishness of the climate and vegetation. Tall elms and green grass have replaced the now familiar eucalyptus trees and tawny uplands, and, indeed, Santiago de Compostela has the reputation for having the dampest climate in all the land of Spain! The Atlantic is near and the great granite paving-stones of the plaza are, more often than not, glistening in the lamp-light each evening, giving it a strangely un-Spanish appearance.

Directly facing the Hostal de los Reyes Catolicos across the Plaza de España stands the Archbishop's Palace which, at first sight, appears to belong to the eighteenth century but, on closer examination, you will find that the great vaulted Sala de Fiestas and its kitchens date from as far back as 1120, and others from 1235–66. On its walls are marvellously carved frescoes depicting the festivities as they were at the end of the Great Pilgrimage 700 or so years ago.

Perhaps one of the most curious buildings in this most curious little city is the collegiate church of Santa Maria de Sar, built between 1133 and 1170, which at some unrecorded time or other decided to sink deeper upon its foundations, but did so in so even a manner that the structure suffered no damage. It contains part of a little-visited cloister, as exquisite as anything to be seen in the great cathedral, with the exception of the Puerta de la Gloria.

There is much more to see, but whether our stay is long or short we must make one final call before we can leave the focal point of the Great Pilgrimage, for centuries the holiest spot in all Europe after Rome itself. This leads us to the Plaza de las Platerias – the Square of the Silversmiths – outside the cathedral's Romanesque portal. Here we shall find the symbol of the pilgrimage accomplished – the scallop-shell of St James the Apostle, fashioned delicately in silver; the amulet to be carried with you through all future journeys, even the last.

25 *Palace of the Marqueses, Villafranca del Bierzo*

9. 'Rias' and Ghosts: Galicia, Asturias and 'La Montaña'

Some years ago, after visiting Santiago de Compostela and most of its 46 churches, my then insatiable curiosity led me on still farther west to Cape Finisterre – Land's End or, until the discovery of America, World's End – but I found that single visit quite enough.

As soon as I had left the quiet green hills that enfold the Pilgrimage City, and crossed the mediaeval bridge that spans the river at Noya – itself a pleasant enough little fishing port built at the head of a deep ria – one becomes sharply aware of the latent threat of the open Atlantic. The road that winds on from there, through Muros to Concorbión, hemmed in by bleak cliffs rising to 2,000 feet, reveals the gigantic violence that, through the ages, has blasted this northwesternmost corner of continental Europe until it begins to oppress the mind unless, of course, the weather is being exceptionally benign. The only tale that the land here has to tell is the story of survival against the hostile elements, and all that is left is a bleak and desolate heritage.

Concorbión, from whence you dive down to the poverty-stricken village of Cape Finisterre itself – the Promontorium Nerium of the Romans – stands, like Noya, at the head of a ria, but is flanked by two dismantled forts, revealing that it once played a part in greater events than the catching of fish. In fact it witnessed Admiral Anson's crushing defeat of the French fleet under La Jonqueira in 1747, and was the point at which Admiral Strachan overtook the battered remnants of the Franco–Spanish fleet seeking escape after Trafalgar in 1805.

Only a little farther north, at Camariñas, there is a rather grim little graveyard containing the bodies of most of the crew of HMS *Serpent*, which went to the bottom in times of peace, but at the height of a gale, as comparatively recently as 1890 – but these are all tales of the angry sea, not of the land, which lies barren and silent under the threat of the ocean.

But, if you like this kind of thing, you will find, on friendly days at least, a suggestion of southern Ireland or the western isles of Scotland – a haunting sense of being upon the fringe of the fabulous. This is not just an attack of Celtic Twilight on my part, but some compound of immense space and timelessness, of shadows on the sea that might be legendary islands, of a dreamy, misty sun, and the vague haze that, between breaths, can turn the familiar scene into something wholly strange.

On this particular journey the prospect did not accord with the peaceful mood induced by three days in Santiago de Compostela, so I drove due north to La Coruña which, for some reason or other, we seem to prefer to call Corunna. Like Cadiz, it is built upon a promontory, heavily defended by picturesque, obsolete stone forts, such as that of Castillo de San Anton and Castillo de San Diego, though it is popularly known as the City of Crystal because of its hundreds of sun-windows facing the port.

Since my last visit I found that the Plaza de Riazor had been 'developed' into an attractive sand bathing-beach, with most of the trimmings, intended to attract the surprisingly large number of people who consider the northern Atlantic as ever being of a temperature suitable for swimming. As, personally, I like the water I swim in to be just off the boil, I was not much tempted.

Also as in Cadiz the narrow streets of the Ciudad Vieja and the lower town are the liveliest and, together with Cadiz, it owes its origin to those ubiquitous sea-traders the Phoenicians.

The Romans, who took possession in 60 B.C., named it Ardobicum Corunium, and the Moors overran it in the eighth century A.D., but once our old enemy Almanzor had disappeared from the scene in 1002, it remained permanently in Christian hands. The Portuguese occupied the town briefly in 1370 during the anarchic period when John of Gaunt landed there in the hope of becoming King of Castile (his daughter Philippa did, in fact, become a very great Queen of Portugal – but that's another story). It was from La Coruña again that a gloomy Philip II set sail in 1554 to marry the ageing daughter of his father's aunt, Mary Tudor, and to serve his short term as King of England.

From this time England was the port's major preoccupation, for from it, on 26 July 1588, the 130 ships, 2,630 cannon and 27,000 men which constituted the 'Invincible Armada' set out to crush Philip's sister-in-law Elizabeth. The history books of our childhood rightly told us much of English courage in meeting the threat, but few recount the incredible incompetence of the unhappy Duke of Medina Sidonia (pressed into command by the direct order of his king on the death of the experienced old Spanish Admiral Santacruz originally assigned for the task), despite his understandably frantic efforts as a General to evade an overnight transformation into an Admiral who knew absolutely nothing of the ways of the sea.

Medina Sidonia's gigantic failure, in an enterprise in which it seems almost certain that no one could possibly have hoped to succeed, led directly to reprisals against La Coruña less than a year later under Drake and Norreys who, after landing in the harbour and burning down most of the town, drove back a strong relieving Spanish force. The fiery resistance to the English raid was led by a Spanish girl, Maria Pita, who is the still-remembered heroine of the city – this at a time when, as related, the Archbishop of Santiago de Compostela, 60 miles away, was attempting to remove the sacred relics – and, presumably, himself – to a place of greater safety, and earning such a spectacular reproof from the Apostle's tomb!

In a quiet garden you will find the grave of the defeated British General Sir John Moore, who lived just long enough to know that the last of his troops had been safely embarked, but even the ending of the Napoleonic Wars did not bring peace to heroic, battered Coruña. From 1815 until 1820 it became, understandably, strongly anti-monarchist – or at least anti-monarchist as exemplified by the miserable Ferdinand VII – and the French troops of the restored French Bourbons intervened on his behalf. Just for good measure the city managed to get involved in the Carlist War of 1836. Fortunately it escaped the Civil War unscathed.

But despite its long and bloody history La Coruña does not feel old, in the way that so many Spanish towns do, perhaps because of its bright, variable skies, screaming gulls and gardens full of unostentatious flowers. There is no trace of the exotic about it or its hardy seagoing people but, being Spain, even if a slightly battered and unfamiliar Spain, it has its share of twelfth- and thirteenth-century churches, including one dedicated to Santiago (in his warlike, mounted 'Matamoros' guise) fighting at the Battle of Clavijo in the year 845.

Unquestionably the most famous building in La Coruña is the 332 feet high Tower of Hercules which, unfortunately, was outwardly restored in 1791. I fear that the claims on behalf of the Greek god-hero cannot be sustained, nor even that it was set up by the Celtic leader Breogan when he set out to conquer and populate Ireland and parts of Scotland (taking the Gallego bagpipes with him as his secret weapon), and it seems fairly certain that it was built by the Romans as a pharos in the time of the Spanish-born Emperor Trajan, and still serves as one – though, of course, with a somewhat more modern lighting system!

El Ferol del Caudillo is famous, as its name implies, as the birthplace of General Franco (he was, incidentally, destined for the navy, and switched to the army only due to drastic cuts in the Naval Estimates following the Cuban War), but when it was known simply as El Ferol it was famous, if at all, for its magnificent natural harbour and the fact that it was Spain's principal naval arsenal in the north, but I think that few people will find the long, coastal road beyond it particularly rewarding. Should they follow it they will glimpse Estaca de Vares, Spain's most northern extremity, far away on their left, weather (as it rarely does) permitting, and pass through the sheltered little sardine fishing port of Vivero before rejoining that which I followed, west of Ribadeo.

Vivero is delightful, if time and distance are of no importance, and four of the ten gates of its defensive walls still stand, one of them dated 1554 and bearing the escutcheon of Charles V. I remember, from 15 or so years ago, admiring its 12-arched bridge over the mouth of the River Androve and also its ninth-century church of Santa Maria del Campo, but it is a very long way to go unless you are really hell-bent on solitude.

My road from La Coruña, capital city of Galicia, ran east to Betanzos, once the Roman Brigantium Flavium, which stands on a low hill still surrounded with its mediaeval defences. Santa Maria del Azoque dates from the fourteenth–fifteenth century, while fourteenth-century San Francisco contains the imposing tomb of the Conde de Andrade which rests, rather unusually, upon the backs of four white marble boars. Near by is the imposing seventeenth–eighteenth-century Cistercian Monastery of Monfero.

This is still the end of the misty land of Galicia, mild and undramatic, bright with orchards and all the flowers of May, perhaps commonplace but also emotionally undemanding. There is much to see, but few obsessive sightseeing 'musts', with pines on the hillsides and many little streams and rivers neatly flanked by poplars.

I had no particular wish to return to Lugo, so turned northeast to the state-run albergue at Villalba to obtain liquid refreshments for both the car and myself, while the manager obligingly telephoned to make a reservation for me at the equivalent establishment at Ribadeo, where I planned to spend my last night in Galicia.

Although I was still in Galicia, and it is Asturias which is famous for its cider, I felt that there was no point in being fussy about 'frontiers' in such a matter, and soon found a five-litre flagon of it, freshly drawn from the wood, set beside me.

Now cider, if you are feeling rather hot and thirsty, and still have to drive quite a few more miles before reaching your destination, is an admirable drink. However, I have always had my cider – even my draught cider – with at least a very slight 'head' on it (I am not discussing the gassy concoction sometimes sold in small bottles as cider in England, which is as innocent of apples as I am of rich uncles), and when I have taken it completely 'flat', the consequences have been disastrous.

Asturian cider tends to be on the 'flat' side of perfection, so it is often served, as it now was, with two pint-sized glasses, to enable me to pour the liquid from one glass to the other from the greatest possible physical distance, i.e. from above my head in one glass to about knee-level to the other, drinking the contents of the lower glass before the distance-induced fizz should subside.

The manager demonstrated, and I then took over. Unfortunately, among the few things I had not brought along with me on this particular journey were my sou'-wester and my Wellington boots. When I left, therefore, I had drunk about one-half of a litre of excellent cider and was wearing the other four and a half.

Incidentally, Asturian cider produced an unusual and, so far as I know, unreported example of twentieth-century diplomacy some years ago.

Castro's cane sugar workers had always slaked their thirst by copious draughts of Asturian cider ever since the days when Cuba was Spanish but, with the advent of Fidel Castro, diplomatic and commercial relations between Spain and Cuba ceased to exist. Russian vodka did not constitute a satisfactory substitute, making the workers either hopelessly drunk or else sleepy in the tremendous heat of the Cuban sun. Finally, despite a few shootings *pour encourager les autres*, it reached the point of 'no cider; then very little sugar or tobacco' – as near to a strike as a free Communist country could hope to achieve – and not only Castro wanted that sugar and those Havana cigars but, far more serious, so did his paymasters, in order to obtain foreign exchange.

What to do? First, President Tubman of Liberia, after a state visit to Madrid, suddenly decided that the good citizens of Monrovia really should drink more Asturian cider, but the order he placed for it was so large that he felt obliged to sell 90 per cent of it to his old friend Fidel in Cuba. Simultaneously, the régime currently in charge in Haiti decided that Papa Doc's brilliant economy had proved so sound that the inhabitants could easily afford to switch from marijuana to Havana cigars, and, through an intermediary, ordered all that Señor Castro could supply though, after a few weeks, this was felt to be detrimental to their health, so he was pleased, through an intermediary, to sell them to Spain. Russia obliged Cuba by buying the increased output of sugar, and everyone concerned was happy, and opened new private numbered bank accounts in Zurich.

Pondering thus upon the wonders of high diplomacy I came to the sleepy little town of Mondoñedo, which I had visited once before, many years ago.

I felt that the sacristan sniffed in a rather marked manner at the light mist of evaporating cider with which I was still enfolded, but he permitted me to enter the thirteenth-century church, with its four sixteenth-century side chapels, so that I was able once more to admire the wood carving of the Virgin and six seraphs smuggled here to safety from St Paul's Cathedral in London at the time of the Reformation – the Old St Paul's, of course, of before the Great Fire.

At Ribadeo I found messages from my very old friend Max Borrell, the wisest man in Spain in all matters pertaining to fishing and shooting (or hunting as our American cousins prefer to call it) telling me not to bother with the River Narcea, or even with the usually easier River Eo, but that 'the salmon on the River Deva, near the albergue at Potes were becoming a positive menace to all other river traffic, and would I come and help to thin them out'! This simplified my plans, so that, leaving early the next day, I set out to follow the coast road to Oviedo, capital of Asturias, and once the last desperate stronghold of Christian Spain.

But before making for Oviedo I had an uncomfortable appointment to keep at the small, hidden village of Cudillero. It is in a cup in the land, deliberately chosen in the vain hope of escaping raids from Norman pirates by its invisibility from the near-by sea. Even today farmyard animals are stabled in lofts, entered from higher up on the same road that passes the front door!

It is a very haunted little town, abounding with *curanderos* anxious to inflict, or parry the misfortunes of the Evil Eye but, after dark, one and all, *curanderos* and inhabitants, carefully avoid the Calle del Trasgu, or Ghost Road, that leads to the cemetery. For there, if you are unlucky, you may still meet the marching 'Santa Compania' – the sheeted dead – always led by a living man who, if he wishes to survive, will carry a cup of holy water and a candle. The 'Holy Company' – called the Güestia – can only be seen by a child, and any adult who does so will die within the year. I stood there for a while, and even in the light of day it is an eerie place and, suddenly, there reached me, strongly and unmistakably, the smell of candle-wax, though there was no one within a couple of hundred yards, and the hair on the back of my neck rose. I do not recommend Cudillero as a place to spend the night.

Asturias is the great Spanish coal and iron-mining centre, and although the pits are not visible in Oviedo itself, one does not in these days go to coalmining centres in search of beauty or happy, smiling faces. Even apart from being sacked by Marshals Ney and Bonnet in 1809 it suffered badly when it attempted to rebel against the Spanish Republic in 1934 – as Catalonia did – but it also underwent a grim siege, by an over-whelmingly large Italian army in 1936–7, at the beginning of the Civil War. Then only 14 of its 60,000 houses were left standing.

But before all these disasters overtook it, it was known as Oviedo 'El Santo' ('The Holy City of Oviedo' or 'Holy Oviedo'), and it was a major detour from the conventional Pilgrim's Way to Santiago de Compostela. The principal reason for its hon-orific surname was that, as the Moors overran more and more of the country, sacred relics were brought here from all over the country for safe-keeping and, it appears, the owners never got them back again!

Today relics, however holy, do not inspire the same degree of devotion, even among Catholics, as they did in the first 1,300 years or so after the Saint–Queen Helena, mother of the Emperor Constantine the Great, started the fashion for them in the fourth century.

The cathedral, despite some fine stained glass is, one feels, a dead shell, with a few real treasures to see but, without inten-tional irreverence, also a great deal of 'junk'. Among the treas-ures is a superb sixteenth-century retable, and the ruthlessly restored pantheon of one of the very earliest of the Spanish kings, Alonso II, who died in 843. However, it is worth persisting as far as the 'Camara Santa', which includes part of the original early ninth-century church, and the equally ancient Capilla de San Miguel, with its rough-hewn capitals and semi-circular vault, whose sturdy antiquity commands respect.

The so-called sacred relics in the chapel of the treasury were saved from the French by sacrificing the cathedral's massive gold and silver plate. They include such mildly unlikely items as one of St Peter's sandals, two thorns from Christ's Crown, one of the 30 pieces of silver paid to Judas for his betrayal, the Holy Shroud – displayed to pilgrims on Good Friday and again on 14 and 15 September – the heart of St Bartholomew, a bone of Moses, a piece of the True Cross, a fragment of the bread with which the multitude were fed following the Miracle of the Loaves and Fishes, the Holy Ark – made of dark oak inlaid with silver plates and brought here in 735, constructed by the Apostles who fled from Jerusalem into Egypt – and some strands of Mary Magdalene's hair! Incidentally, by far the most interesting thing about the Ark – whether or not you accept its authenticity – is the stone upon which it stands, an object of veneration for at least 1,200 years, revealing the carved features and expressions of the Apostles themselves.

These relics have been profoundly reverenced here for well over a thousand years, and some of them are beautiful aesthetically, so I will not discuss their credibility now, but I fear that I contemplated them unmoved. Indeed, if mine had been the choice between their preservation and the cathedral's magnificent gold and silver plate at the beginning of last century, I should have been sorely tempted to let them go and, if you have read as far as this, you will realise that, where things so ancient are concerned, I am usually to be found on the side of the angels!

However, there is no questioning the authenticity of the early ninth-century Maltese Cross, adorned with gold filigree and many precious stones, and the even older Cruz de la Victoria carried into the Battle of Covadonga by Pelayo, first King of Asturias, in 718.

If time permits there are two strange churches near Oviedo of immense age, Santa Maria de Naranco and San Miguel de

Lillo, both dating from the ninth century and both still in use. The latter, which stands in a forested glade, has arrow slits instead of windows, placed there, quite obviously, for no sacerdotal reason, but for use in discouraging evilly intentioned raiding Moors! It is in some respects unique as a church, as its door jambs bear late Roman and early Visigothic designs.

But, to be honest, Oviedo is one of the very few places in Spain where I do not feel at ease. Antiquity, as you will perhaps have noticed, both soothes and stimulates me. Somehow all these 'sacred relics' seem, for me, vaguely inimical. Perhaps I could still smell about them a whiff of that same ghostly candle wax that had snatched away my tranquillity in Cudilleros. This is the land of the *Xamas,* or misleading water sprites, who are free to slip their changeling children into unguarded cradles on the eve of the feast of St John, when their wailing voices can be heard – not prophesying death like Irish banshees – but troubling the sleep of those whose house they approach.

Certainly this is the land of the race of *vaqueiros,* who are tangible and very much of this earth, who drive their cattle down to the villages from high summer pasturages, yodelling cowboys who have always lived outside any community except their own, in primitive thatched cottages high on the almost trackless mountainsides. Like gipsies, they are not allowed to stand inside the main body of the church, nor to receive Communion at the altar rails, only at the church door, and their dead are buried in a carefully segregated section of the graveyard. No one seems to know much about them; they are just another of the many mysteries of the hidden Spain.

The slight feeling of restlessness, which always afflicts me in Oviedo, decided me to push on into the familiar mountains to the south, and the even more familiar, even if slightly Spartan security of the parador which lies at 3,800 feet above sea level, where I had once spent a happy holiday in the 1950s. However, I do not advise anyone to take this road unless they are going to Leon, as it is a terrific climb through savagely wild country, but I remembered the road well, and was rewarded when, still short of the Pass at Pajares I saw three brown bears – father, mother and junior – who had decided to cross the road.

I stopped politely and signalled them to pass, and had a good look at them from some 15 feet or so. Papa must have been about four feet tall; Mama (to whom I had not been formally introduced) haughtily refused to admit my existence, and junior made rude faces at me. My second reward was that the parador remembered me kindly, and gave me a marvellous meal despite the lateness of the hour. My third came in the morning, when I could see the whole vast amphitheatre of mountains, up to 7,800 feet Mount Ubiña, in all their majesty, and not, as I knew from experience they often were, shrouded in fog caused by the heat of the Spanish plateau behind me meeting the cool, moist air of the Atlantic.

It was a pleasant caprice to have come, but I was way off my intended route – at least I had finally rid myself of the scent of ghostly candles!

The trouble is that Pajares Pass is just what it claims to be – a pass through the Cantabrian mountains linking Oviedo and Leon – the once great cities of the pilgrimage, until the mal-practices of the Asturian bandits did away with what was called the 'Oviedo Deviation', and the human stream kept firmly on its way towards the Tomb of the Apostle, south of the main mountain range. Only between the loveless mining towns of Pola de Lena and Mieres could I find an abominable track to lead me back into the anything but straight if narrow way from which my unrehearsed night at the parador had seduced me. My real objective had always been Cangas de Onis and Covadonga, which is a perfectly simple run from Oviedo – I had just made it difficult for myself by gallivanting off into the mountains.

Cangas de Onis is associated with the dawn of the Recon-quest – though a more suitable name would be the Resistance, in the World War Two sense of the word. After the rout of the Christian Goths and Visigoths, and the death in battle of King Roderick in 711 on the banks of the River Guadalete, not far from Cadiz, a number of disunited bands from the defeated army found their way – or were forced by Moorish harassment – into this northern corner of the country, protected by the mountain barrier provided by the Cantabrian Range.

The Visigothic kings had always been elected, not hereditary

– one of their fundamental weaknesses, as the other leading men seemed always to have been jealous of the lucky one – but now the outstanding personality among them was clearly a knight named Pelayo or, according to some sources, Pelagius. But it was certainly no court over which he presided when he made his headquarters in this tranquil valley near the head of the River Deva.

Still, when the inevitable news came, in 718, that a force of 6,000 Moors had been detached to wipe out the Christian remnant on their northern flank, it was Pelayo who led his 300 knights to meet them in the mountain gorge of Covadonga and, after the total destruction of the Moorish force, he was created King on the field of battle. Although the forces engaged in the Battle of Covadonga today seem small, the defeat was sufficiently severe to decide the Moors, temporarily at least, to abandon the conquest of the extreme north, and to press on towards what was to be their second great reverse, at the hands of Charles Martel at Poitiers, 14 years later.

This gave the little Asturian kingdom time to consolidate itself and, later, to thrust from behind its mountain defences to liberate Leon, and then Burgos.

Cangas de Onis was the first 'capital' of the Asturian kings, though it is little more than an obscure village today, notable chiefly for the Chapel of the Holy Cross (Santa Cruz) built on a Celtic tumulus by Pelayo's immediate successor King Favila in 735, though there is an attractive thirteenth-century bridge over the River Sella if one can drag oneself out of the mists of the ages to appreciate such relative modernity!

The gorge itself, and the Santa Cueva, are regarded by Spaniards as the cradle of their history, and there is a pilgrimage to Nuestra Señora de las Batallas ('Our Lady of Battles') on September 8 which, as a foreigner, you should try to avoid, together with the Holy Cave itself, where the River Deva bursts from the mountainside.

The Cueva itself is the point where Pelayo chose to make his final resistance to the Moorish attack, and is little more than an arched recess, which today may be approached by a flight of marble steps or, alternatively, through a long tunnel from the terrace of the nineteenth-century basilica which, despite its modernity, is not displeasing, and replaces one built by Alfonso I* in the eighth century, but destroyed by fire in 1777.

In the cave wall is the sarcophagus of Pelayo, who died in 737, and his wife, Gaudiosa, while at the back of the chapel are those of Pelayo's sister Ermesinda and her husband Alfonso I – third king of the Asturian line.

There is nothing very impressive about Covadonga, and no doubt it looked much the same when Pelayo and his 300 knights rode out to meet their fate and found a kingdom on that distant day – a peaceful, green mountain valley, with little to distinguish it from a dozen such places on the fringes of the Picos de Europa. Pelayo and his followers ride in the mists of time; little or nothing is known of their looks or ways, and only a very faint echo of their dedicated faith can perhaps be caught across the gulf of nearly 13 centuries.

Beyond Covadonga the rough road climbs only a little farther, to the icy waters of Lake Enol and the Lago de la Ercina – both lifeless and slightly sinister. There the way is barred absolutely by the trackless Picos de Europa, the really wild eastern spur of the Cantabrian Mountains, rising to nearly 9,000 feet, the free home of chamois – saved from extinction by Alfonso XIII – brown bear (such as we met on our fleeting trip to Pajares), wild cat, wolf, osprey, imperial eagles and a wealth of other wild life found in few other places in present-day Europe and yet, oddly enough, one of the nature reserves least explored by the growing number of wildlife enthusiasts.

So I was forced to return through Cangas de Onis, and then turn east again, along the coast road to San Vicente de la Barqueira, to which in any case I had been specially recommended – and rightly so.

It is an extraordinarily picturesque little seaport, surrounded on three sides by tidal rivers, so that you must enter it by the 28-arched Puente de la Maza, built in 1433, which leads you directly to the thirteenth-century church, containing the un-

---

* There is a division of opinion about the use of Alfonso or Alonso for the Kings of Asturias, and it is not until the eleventh century that Alonso was definitely abandoned in favour of Alfonso, which somehow sounds more Spanish. C.S.

comfortably realistic reclining effigy of the Grand Inquisitor Antonio Corro. Looking at those calm features, it is difficult not to wonder how many poor creatures he had seen fit 'to release to the secular arm' – the polite euphemism that condemned the victim to be burned to death.

As it is precisely at the point where rivers become brackish – and San Vicente, as already mentioned, had no less than three from which to choose – that the delicious *angula** (to be served '*a la bilbaina*') is to be found, I felt that I had but to seach to find this greatest of all fishy delights and, ultimately, I was successful, though only after a particularly bizarre accident.

There are some lovely sixteenth- and seventeenth-century private mansions in San Vicente, and it was while I was wandering along a street of these, having parked the car in a safe place, that I heard inexplicable noises – I hesitate to call it music – and, turning a corner, found that I was, quite accidentally, involved in a funeral, or rather in a 'wake'. It was quite informal, and there were no signs of grief or mourning and, as I had stopped, I was motioned inside.

My heart slipped a beat however when I found that the coffin had been placed in the centre of a little entrance patio, and that everyone, including myself, was expected to dance slowly around it. That was odd enough, but then I noticed that in addition to dancing, everyone was *buzzing* like a hive of bees! I have never had difficulty in falling in with local customs in out of the way places in Spain, or indeed anywhere else, but I could not help feeling that there really was something distinctly odd in finding myself gravely dancing *and* buzzing round a corpse to which, as it were, I had never even been introduced!

Backing away unobstrusively I found my restaurant only a few hundred yards away, and although the meal that followed – scalding hot *angulas* still bubbling in the finest oil, though accompanied by an unbroken clove of garlic, served in the earthenware dish in which they had been cooked, and eaten

---

* *angulas*: literally 'elvers', which are also found in the upper reaches of the River Severn but – perish the thought – never eaten there! c.s.

with a wooden fork – was fully up to expectation, the explanation of the buzzing-dancing 'wake' was not. The fisherman, whose wife served my delicious food, had known the dead man well, so I enquired tactfully just what the ceremony I had glimpsed signified. I had guessed that it was a 'wake', but apparently it was one held before, instead of after taking the body to church for a normal Christian burial. I then led on to the unusual 'music' of the buzzing. What, I asked, did it signify?

'Ah,' said my informant, 'that was the bees' – then added quickly, 'but, of course, the *white* bees.'

This did not help much, but I tried again, pointing out the fact that I had been to quite a number of funerals and 'wakes' in various parts of the world, but had never previously heard the mourners buzz – and why white bees instead of the usual variety? He seemed a little surprised at my ignorance, and said that such ceremonies were common all along the coast though, he admitted, more universally so in Asturias and Galicia, whence the dead man came. The white bees symbolised the good spirits that welcomed that of the dead man, and which could sometimes be clearly seen, by those 'with the sight', rising from the closed coffin.

For once I had to admit myself completely out of my depth, only recalling that I had noticed one or two frescoes in pilgrim churches along the Way which depicted bees around the person of some saint or martyr, so the custom may not be, as I first thought, pagan or pre-Christian – though I have never found a priest able, or anyway willing, to explain the origin of the mystery.

However, I still had before me the task of penetrating the great wall of the Picos de Europa to the south in order to reach my night's remote lodging, and this meant returning the few miles to Unquera.

From there the mountain track twists and climbs through increasingly intimidating scenery, through Panes, where there is an early eleventh-century Mozarabic chapel, to the Hermida Gorge (Desfiladero de la Hermida) to the little town of Potes. It feels like a great deal more, but Potes is only some 23 miles from the coast, and from there the 'road' simply follows the

26 *A typical slum alley, with a typically attractive girl . . .*

infant River Deva until you come to the modest, but very adequate, chalet-style parador. In fact there is a mountain refuge on a 3,300 feet shelf of 8,700 feet high Mount El Cerredo – but this is for the hearty ones, or for the strictly limited number of licensed hunters of the chamonix, and not for the likes of me.

I spent two pleasant days, and grassed two salmon, one of eight pounds and one of ten, but I am a poor salmon fisherman, as I have had too few opportunities to indulge in such an expensive pastime. My two were, perhaps, as my old friend Max occasionally put it, 'just tired of life anyway'!

As I drove back to the coast, heading for the fleshpots of Santander and its surroundings, I remembered the days in the early 1950s when Max had fought to save the dwindling game fish of Spain's mountain streams and rivers and, incidentally, to turn their salvation into a valuable source of foreign exchange, at a time when the country needed it far more than it does today.

From time immemorial the local inhabitants had, understandably, regarded the contents of their rivers as a little, much needed, free food – particularly in Asturias. Unfortunately the average Asturian's idea of a nice day's fishing consisted in lobbing a hand grenade into any promising reach of river, and then collecting the stunned, mutilated and, incidentally, unpleasantly flavoured floating victims. This method, apart from all other considerations, was rapidly depopulating the rivers completely, when Max, as Technical Adviser on Sport to the inspired Director of Turismo the late Luis Bolin, was authorised to take action.

The locals naturally objected violently, and openly threatened that they would shoot Max on sight if he dry-fished 'their' river. Max replied by an advertisement in the local papers (the threats, obviously, carried no postal address for a reply) giving the exact location where he would be fishing at certain equally fixed hours. He added that he would be wearing a scarlet shirt, so that they should have no difficulty whatsoever in spotting him!

He kept his programme and, as so often happens in Spain, the opposition lost all support in face of a gesture of cool courage!

27 Chamois in the Picos de Europa

10. Goodbye to the Basque Country

As we drive east from our foray into the Picos de Europa, a few of them still tipped here and there with snow, we are well back into Castile, or La Montaña as the maritime province of Santander – as distinct from the town itself – is often correctly named. Historically speaking this was Old and New Castile's only and quite narrow opening to the sea. Inland the country still rises, through thickly wooded hills and ancient, stork-nested little stone towns, towards the high plateau with which we became familiar on our way to Santiago de Compostela, but the great mountain mass gradually begins to fall behind us.

From San Vicente de la Barquera the main road swings away from the sea in a short loop through Cabezón de la Sal and Torrelavega and, from there, should you wish to do so, you can completely bypass Santander by making direct for Solares – from whence comes one of Spain's best-known mineral waters – but ours (the worst, as usual, being my choice) follows the coast to Comillas, Santillana del Mar and the prehistoric caves of Altamira.

Comillas is a pleasant little seaside resort, but the village is more or less a memorial to the first Marqués de Comillas who, in the 1880s and 1890s, made a larger fortune than any of his contemporaries in Spain as a shipping magnate and industrial tycoon, but is probably better remembered today – if remembered at all – as the uncle of José Maria Sert, the great muralist and painter, who was judged a worthy boon companion in the *fin de siècle* Parisian circle of Picasso, Toulouse

Lautrec and the rest of their great contemporaries.

Las Cuevas de Altamira, painted some 12,000 or 13,000 years ago, belong to what the experts call the Upper Magdalenian Age, and were only discovered by accident about a century ago, together with a remarkable stalactite grotto about a hundred yards from their entrance.

You may have seen other similar prehistoric cave dwellings, though few are better than these. There are some in France, and many others in Spain, particularly around Teruel for example (though often sadly neglected), where the artist has depicted men as well as animals, though with serpent heads – presumably a tribe whose language the artist could not understand, and so suspected of snake-like cunning and deceit!

In any case, the wall paintings of Altamira are mostly of bison, wild boar and deer, depicted in ochre, outlined by flint scratches, often shaped to the natural curves and formations of the rock, and are well worth visiting, particularly as, since I was last there, better lighting enabled me to enjoy them without acquiring a severe crick in the neck.

Using coloured pigment composed only of charcoal, ochre and haematites, the artists managed to achieve every shade of yellow, red and grey. This was during Europe's last Ice Age, when there was only a narrow strip of ice-free land between the mountains to the south and the Bay of Biscay, and provide remarkable evidence of primitive man's desire, even though they were often only passing nomads, to beautify the cave-homes in which they sheltered from the wild beasts that haunted the outer night. Prehistoric cave paintings may not be your favourite subject (it is not mine), but I never pass this way without a brief visit.

But the reward for having taken this road lies in the little town of Santillana del Mar, though it is a misnomer in that it is at least four miles from the sea.

To get a room at the Parado (or Meson) de Gil Blas is just about impossible without considerable advance booking, and I had succeeded only by invoking more or less Divine Intervention some weeks earlier through the Dirección General del Turismo in Madrid, aided by the fact that even the very end of May is not quite 'The Season' on Spain's northern coast. It is worth the effort if you can be sure of your booking though, if thwarted, it is no great distance to the many excellent hotels of Santander – though, in July and August, Santander, too, has a high season when hotels are full. For now we have left the Hidden Spain – and the Voice of the Packaged Tourist is again heard in the Land.

This proximity to the elegant centre of Spain's yachting, golfing, pigeon-shooting smart set means that during the day a camera-slung horde is briefly in evidence, but when they drive away Santillana del Mar returns unscathed to its true fifteenth–sixteenth-century self with astonishing rapidity.

Gil Blas is a literary character like (though singularly unlike in personality) Cervantes' 'Don Quixote', but there is nothing fanciful about the parador named after him, which is one of the little town's many four- and five-hundred-years-old mansions, complete with flagged stone floors and low oak beams, but it was one of the earliest of the state-operated conversions of beautiful old buildings that would otherwise have crumbled away with neglect, and so was done when there was much less capital available for such enterprises. Perhaps for that reason it avoids the slightly stagey fantasies of the architects later engaged for similar work.

It is comfortable, even if rather expensive since the pound went 'floating', but after my days in the Picos de Europa I unashamedly luxuriated.

When the tourists have gone for the day, take a quiet evening stroll through the old town, and see for yourself the scarlet of geraniums splashing warmth on the grey stone walls beneath the carved armorial bearings of some now forgotten, once powerful family. The streets are cobbled, and between the noble old mansions you will see the beasts of the fields being led slowly home from their day's work and, as often as not, stabled in equally aristocratic surroundings.

Soon – for Santillana del Mar is only a small town – you will come across the imposing Romanesque portal leading into the collegiate church and, beyond it, one of the most peaceful cloisters we have seen in our many days of travel along the north coast. The church contains the tomb of the fourth-century martyr Santa Juliana – Santillana is a corruption of her name – and there is a fine retable dating from 1453 and a solid silver altar.

The whole town has lately been declared a National Monument, so it regains its feeling of timelessness during the quiet hours, and this has been done without altering its authenticity and normal life.

But from Santillana – unless we retrace our steps or turn south to Burgos or, alternatively, to Reinosa, with its strange Celtic disk-shaped stelae – all roads tend to lead to Santander. It is a dual city; part of it a bustling, modern port loading coal for Barcelona and unloading dried cod caught off the banks of Newfoundland, or carrying mixed cargoes and passengers to Cadiz and the Canary Isles. It is a pleasant way to waste an hour, watching all this activity from a seat outside a café on the Paseo de Pereda and sampling the delicious prawns which will be on offer. Santander's second half is the luxury resort, trying to dissociate itself from all these commercial activities, and disguising itself under the name of El Sardinero.

Although Santander claims to have been in existence since the martyrdom of San Celedonio in the year 300 (his body lies in the crypt of the cathedral), the first reliable historical reference to it comes as late as 1068, when it is referred to as the port of San Emerito. It was from here that the Saint–King Ferdinand set out for his successful blockade of Seville in 1248, when the place appears under its present name, and here it was that the Emperor Charles V landed to take possession of his mad mother's kingdom in 1522, together with his Flemish mistress Barbara Blomberg.

Charles was only 22 years old at the time, and Barbara was not only the great love of his strenuous, rather arid life (though, of course, he had other mistresses later), but the liaison is of note also because it produced Don Juan of Austria, victor of the great naval battle of Lepanto, which broke effective Turkish control of the western basin of the Mediterranean. Doña Barbara lies buried not far east of Santander at the little port of Santoña.

Then, again, our own King Charles I sailed from here for England, with Buckingham, in 1623, after his slightly farcical wooing of Philip IV's sister, and Napoleon's Marshal Soult

sacked the city in 1808, but its ties with Spain's historic past
are few and tenuous. Latterly it became the more aristocratic
alternative to San Sebastian under the auspices of the Queen
Regent, Maria Cristina, and the young Alfonso XIII.

The cathedral need not delay you, in this nation of magnificent cathedrals, the only impressive thing about it being the
vaulted, early Gothic crypt below it, dating from the first years
of the fourteenth century.

Santander's greatest years were those when the city presented the young king with the little Palacio Real on the
promontory known as La Magdalena, and it became his and his
English Queen's favourite summer home. These were in the
happy days before either the ravages of haemophilia, bequeathed by Queen Victoria to her grand-daughter, or the in-
evitability of a Civil War, and death in exile, had cast their
shadows over the lives of the attractive young couple. Today
the little palace is the venue for one of those half-holiday, half-
educative international summer university courses, and has not
gained in attractiveness from the change.

El Sardinero has two splendid sand bathing beaches – or,
more precisely, one very long beach divided by a rocky promontory – and a third below the Sporting Club. Its really beautiful golf course is Spain's equivalent of Scotland's 'Royal and
Ancient' at St Andrews; pigeon-shooting competitions (which I
dislike as, with experts, it is about six to one against the
pigeon's survival) for impressive silver cups and, above all, it is
Spain's yachting equivalent to Cowes. It even has a casino,
though since the abolition of gambling – except, of course, in
the endless state lotteries and, latterly, the football pools – it
has degenerated into a club. Yachting, international tennis
tournaments, horse-racing, boxing and, needless to say, almost
daily bullfights during its 'Semana Grande', from 25 July until 2
August, are the order of the day – every day.

Golf, once reputedly only for the rich, and rapidly returning
to that position, has always been taken seriously in Santander
and, somewhat later, at the Puerta de Hierro Club just outside
Madrid, but it is, except for a few excellent professionals, a
product of snob-appeal – like the French 'le five o'clock',
meaning tea. I speak from long experience and, unless you are

a 'natural' at the game, the chief qualities required for the playing of adequate golf are humility, to prevent lifting the head, and self-restraint, and both are qualities heartily despised by 99 per cent of the entire Spanish people, female as well as male!

I do not wish to be unjust to the pleasures of Santander (or El Sardinero), but it does not provide the kind of holiday which I can usually afford and, when I can afford it, not the one that I choose in preference to several alternatives. So, without too much regret I left this slightly overdressed atmosphere, and headed for a brief look at Laredo.

Again I found superb bathing conditions, and there is a great fiesta there during the second half of August, which culminates in a terrific Battle of Flowers. Here, as in what was my home town of Sitges, in Cataluña, for several years, they produce the intricately designed carpets of flower petals for the Fiesta of Corpus Cristi which, on a certain occasion, provided me with an unforgettable memory.

I was walking along the narrow pavement, admiring the ingenuity of the designs, a little way behind a middle-aged English couple, whose pleasure at the beauty of the petal pictures was certainly genuine, even if a little naïve. The woman, happily flitting from one to the other, came to a representation of a chalice containing the Sacrament, and could bear it no more, turning to her sturdy spouse with the cry,

'But look Len, did you ever see anything so cute? A cup for them to drink their "vino" ' – a giggle fully excused this rather naughty use of a foreign word – and then, pointing to a representation of the Host, she gaily continued, 'and a genuine Spanish pancake to go with it!' Then dropping her voice discreetly, she added, 'That's all they can get, I suppose, under a Fascist régime.'

From Laredo you can look across the bay to Santoña (which some Spaniards like to style 'The Gibraltar of the North') where, as already told, the young Emperor Charles V had landed finally to claim his tremendous heritage. It was here, in Laredo, that he landed 34 years later, a prematurely worn out old man of 56, bound on his last journey towards voluntary abdication, and to welcome death at the Monastery of Yuste. It would have been strange if on this occasion he had not looked across the bay, as I was now doing, and compared his two landings. Barbara was to outlive him by many years but, perhaps, on his way to Yuste, he was doing his best to forget his youthful peccadillos. At least he presented two magnificent bronze lecterns, in the form of Imperial Eagles, to Laredo's church, but it seems that he never returned again to Santoña, with its fragrant memories.

Having planned only a short day's run, with the magnificent parador of Santurce for the night as my objective, I spent a pleasant hour in Castro Urdiales. Although it had suffered a little 'tidying up' since I had last seen it, it is still one of the most charming, as it is also one of the oldest of the many small port towns along this coast.

Once the Roman Flaviobriga, it was destroyed by raiding Vikings, though the *castro*, or fort, survived in its little creek of Urdiales, from above which the modern lighthouse today flashes its eternal warnings into the night. I found the ochre-coloured Gothic church of Nuestra Señora de la Anunciación rewarding and, as I settled down to my giant grilled prawns (with a very hot red pepper in fine oil as a sauce) I recalled with pleasure – he was one of my schoolboy heroes – that poor, broken Cesar Borgia had found succour here, at least for a while, after his desperate escape from imprisonment in the Castle of La Mota, near Medina del Campo, in one of the two now ruined monasteries behind Castro Urdiales.

As I continued my lunch with *callos a la madrillena* it was as well that the local *chacoli* is dry, white and of low alcoholic content and available in bulk, thus averting a possible case of spontaneous combustion. I hoped that while he was nominal lord of the town, from 1366 to 1370, the Black Prince had refrained from such gastronomic orgies while staying at the now ruined College of the Knights Templar.

Still it was only a short way from there to the parador at Santurce, which is an excellent place to stay if you are making use of the practical, and rather reasonable car ferry services which connect Bilbao and Southampton or if, as in my case (while fully recognising its importance as the Basque 'capital') you find it an exceptionally dreary town.

If you should tire of the vigorous commercial life of Bilbao and its blast furnaces, you may discover that the capital of Vizcaya has a surprisingly rich art gallery. I passed a pleasant hour looking at fifteenth-century Florentine and Flemish old masters; four superb El Grecos; assorted canvases by Velazquez, Zurbarán, Ribera and a Goya portrait of the little nymphomaniac monkey-faced Queen Luisa de Palma, wife of Carlos IV, as good as anything in Madrid's Prado.

But I could not readily end any kind of a pilgrimage to Santiago de Compostela in Bilbao, however superficially I might have observed its religious significance, so, ignoring both the seaside charms of Zumaya, and the Edwardian pleasures of San Sebastian, I headed once more for Pamplona for my last night in Spain.

Then, very early next day, I again reached the head of the Pass of Roncesvalles and, leaving the car, paused for a little while and looked back, my shadow elongated before me by the early sun from France.

There stretched away before me the 350 miles to Santiago, which the pilgrims of earlier days used to walk in 13 full days – some 27 miles a day, on the days which were not Sundays or Saints' Days, which were also days of rest and religious devotion, or in main centres of the Faith along the road, such as Burgos and Leon.

Most came through this often misty pass in the mountain barrier of the Pyrenees, and they came from all over the Christian world. Many died: none were ever afterwards quite the same, even the vast majority who safely returned to their homes, for they believed profoundly that they had earned a strong claim to eternal life. They had journeyed west to the end of the road; the end of the world, Finis Terre; to the limits of life itself, often with death as their companion, in a kind of rehearsal and preparation for death. Most had been sent back to live out the lives to which they had been destined; a few had continued the journey beyond the limits of the known world, which is death.

King and queens; mighty generals and almost hopeless freedmen; gipsies and *juglares*; saints and sinners, had all paused here, solemn when confronted by the reality of their great undertaking; many in fear, a few in exaltation, but all face to face with something which they knew was going to test them to the limits of their physical and spiritual strength.

As I drove down the winding road towards St Jean Pied de Port in France the sun was brilliant, and the fields full of bright flowers.

Index